FAYR

Piano - Vocal

RODGERS AND HART

A MUSICAL ANTHOLOGY

ISBN 0-88188-337-9

HAL•LEONARD™
CORPORATION
7777 W. Bluemound Rd. P.O. Box 13819 Milwaukee, WI 53213

Richard Rodgers and Lorenz Hart

FOREWORD

By DOROTHY RODGERS

Dick and Larry wrote a prodigious number of songs between 1925 and 1943, the years of their collaboration, and the greatest output was in the decade of the thirties. I remember so well coming home in the late afternoons and knowing, from the moment I stepped out of the elevator into our small private entrance hall, that the all too-pervasive scent of Larry's Uppmann cigar meant that Dick and Larry had been, or possibly still were, working. They never seemed to mind my interrupting them to let them know I was home, and sometimes if they were excited about a new song that they had just finished, Dick would play the melody while Larry sang the lyric. Larry's voice was not musical, but there is always something special about the way a composer or lyricist presents his own work, and Larry could make the listener aware of the feeling and mood of the song. If Larry wasn't around, Dick liked to play the accompaniment while he whistled the tune, and he would have me follow the lyric by reading it silently. Since I have, what Dick in his wonderfully understated style of humor would refer to as, "a small but disagreeable voice," I was pleased when he would let me recite the lyric while he played the song for friends. I cared so much about getting the lyrics across that Dick claimed he actually liked my rendition!

In my mind's eye, I can see Larry, leaning against the wall of our living room, scribbling the lyric in soft black pencil on yellow foolscap. His head, the paper and the lyric were all slanted uphill. One day I walked into the room to find Larry standing in front of the huge studio window with a large lighted cigar in his mouth, totally unaware that he was burning an enormous hole in the curtain. Whenever anything of that kind happened, Larry's apologies were so abject that I usually ended up feeling that it was somehow my fault.

The question most frequently asked of Dick and Larry — and, I suspect, of all song-writing collaborators — was, "Which comes first, the words or the music?" Dick always felt it was a most sensible question, and there were several serious answers to it, depending on the circumstances. With Larry, Dick always had to write the music first because it was the only way he could get Larry to work. (And even then he had to stay in the room while Larry was writing to make sure he didn't disappear!) In Dick's collaboration with Oscar Hammerstein II, the situation was quite different. Oscar liked the freedom of being able to write the lyric first, and he would work in his home either in Doylestown, Pennsylvania, or in New York. He worked carefully, slowly and meticulously, and only after he and Dick had fully discussed exactly what they wanted to accomplish with a particular song, was the neatly typed manuscript delivered to Dick who would attack it eagerly and set the words to music. Dick found it just as simple to write either way, and when he wrote both music and lyrics for "No Strings" after Oscar died, he used both methods — and sometimes even wrote music and lyrics simultaneously.

This songbook has many of my favorite Rodgers and Hart songs, and if they should turn out to be among your favorites, too, I'm sure you will enjoy hearing them again. For those of you to whom the songs will be new, I hope you will become new Rodgers and Hart fans.

Dorothy Rodgers

May, 1984

Rodgers & Hart

SHOWS

Rodgers & Hart
SONGS

I've Got Five Dollars

Music by RICHARD RODGERS
Lyric by LORENZ HART

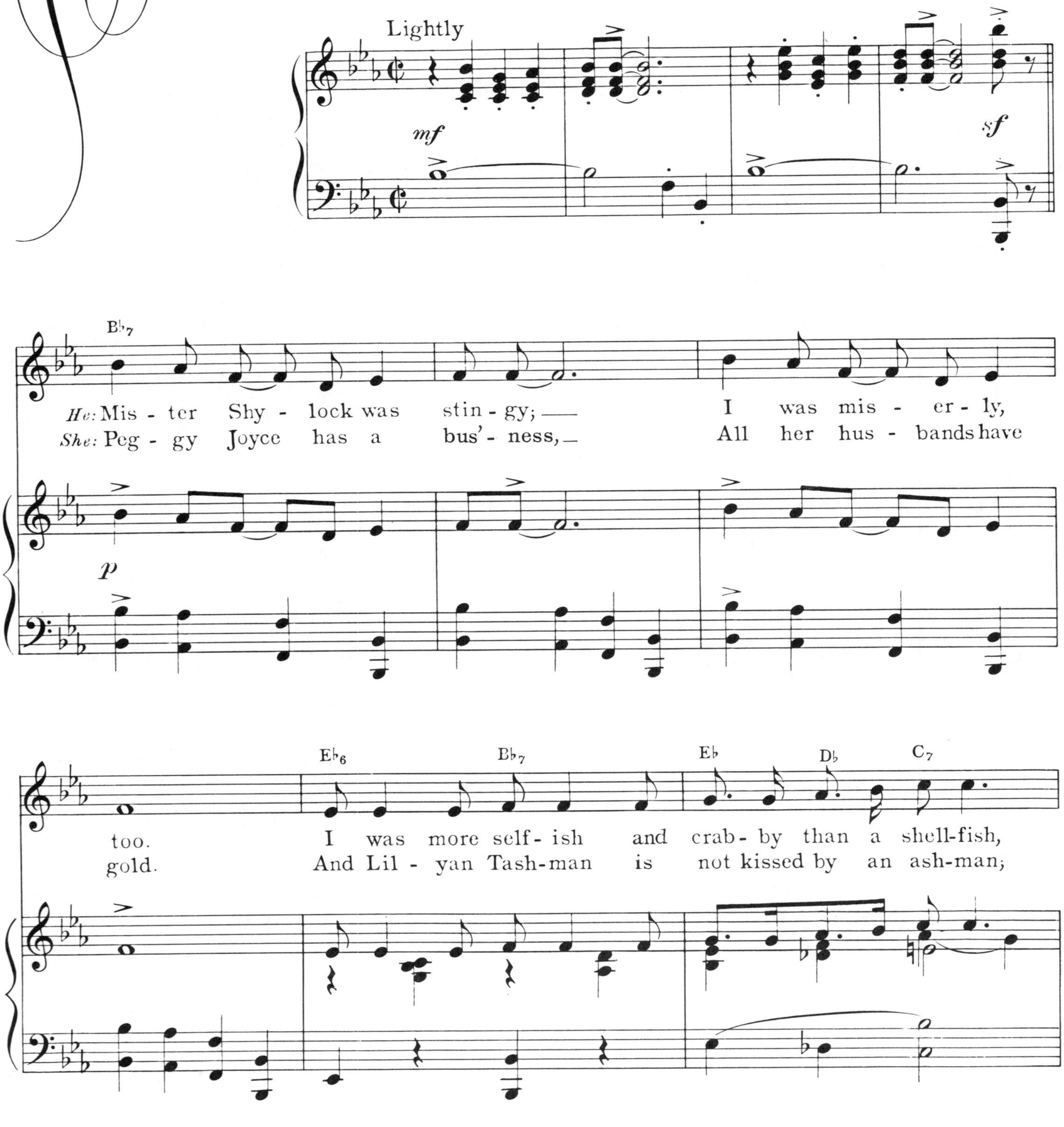
Lightly
mf
sf
B♭7
He: Mis - ter Shy - lock was stin - gy; — I was mis - er - ly,
She: Peg - gy Joyce has a bus' - ness, — All her hus - bands have
p
E♭6
B♭7
E♭
D♭
C7
too. I was more self - ish and crab - by than a shell-fish,
gold. And Lil - yan Tash - man is not kissed by an ash - man;

Fm7 B♭7 A♭ E♭ F7
Oh dear,_ it's queer_ What love_ can do!
But now,_ some-how_ Wealth leaves me cold.
B♭7 A♭ F7(♭5) B♭7 B♭+
I'd give all_ my pos- ses- sions for you:_
Though you're poor as a church mouse I'm sold!_
Refrain (leisurely)
E♭ Fm7 B♭7 E♭
He: I've got five dol-lars; I'm in good con-
She: I've got five dol-lars; Eight-y five re-
p
Fm7 B♭7 E♭ Fm7 B♭7 E♭
di-tion; And I've got am-bi-tion; That be-longs to
la-tions; Two lace com-bi-na-tions; They be-long to

B♭7 E♭ Fm7 B♭7 E♭
you; Six shirts and col-lars; Debts be - yond en -
you! Two coats with col-lars; Ma and Grand-ma
Fm7 B♭7 E♭ Fm7 B♭7 E♭
dur-ance On my life in - sur-ance, That be-longs to
wore 'em; All the moths a - dore 'em; They be-long to
G♭ B♭7 A♭ E♭
you; I've got a heart That
you; I've got two lips That
mp dolce
B♭7 E♭ Fm7 B♭7 E♭
must be spurt-in'! Just be cer-tain
care for mat - ing, There-fore wait-ing

Cm7 F7 B♭7 E♭ Fm7 B♭7
I'll be true! Take my five dol-lars!
will not do! Take my five dol-lars!
p
E♭ Fm7 B♭7 E♭ B♭m6 C7
Take my shirts and col-lars! Take my heart that hol-lers,
Take my coats and col-lars! Take my heart that hol-lers,
F7 A♭7 1. E♭ Cm7 D♭9 F7(♭5) B♭7
"Ev-'ry-thing I've got be-longs to you!"
"Ev-'ry-thing I've got be-longs to you!"
cresc.
mf
2. E♭
you!"
you!"
mf
L.H.
f
sf
8
Led.

I Wish I Were In Love Again

Words by LORENZ HART
Music by RICHARD RODGERS

Moderately
mf
G
C
A7
D7
C
You don't know that I felt good
When we up and part - ed.
p
G
C
A7
D7
You don't know I knocked on wood,
C
Bm
Glad - ly bro - ken heart - ed.
Wor - ry - ing is through, I

Am7 D7 G Em7 A7 D7
sleep all night,__ Ap - pe - tite and health re - stored.
G C A7 D7 G♯dim D7
You don't know how much I'm bored!
G A♯dim G
The sleep - less nights, The dai - ly fights, The quick to - bog - gan when you
fur - tive sigh, The black - ened eye, The words "I'll love you till the
p–mf
A♯dim G A♯dim
reach the heigths; I miss the kiss - es and I miss the bites, I
day I die," The self - de - cep - tion that be - lieves the lie, I

D7 C#dim D7 D7sus G A#dim
wish I were in love a-gain! The bro-ken dates, The end-less waits, The
wish I were in love a-gain! When love con-geals It soon re-veals The
G A#dim G
love-ly lov-ing and the hate-ful hates, The con-ver-sa-tion with the
faint a-rom-a of per-form-ing seals, The dou-ble cross-ing of a
A#dim D7 G7
fly-ing plates, I wish I were in love a-gain!
pair of heels I wish I were in love a-gain!
C Cm G E+ A7 D7 G G7
No more pain, No more strain,
No more care, No de-spair.
mf

C
Cm
G
E+
A7
Now I'm sane, but I would rath - er be
I'm all there now, But I'd rath - er be
D7
G
A#dim
ga - ga! The pulled out fur of cat and cur, The
punch - drunk! Be - lieve me sir, I much pre - fer The
p
G
A#dim
G
fine mis - mat - ing of a him and her, I've learned my les - son, but I
clas - sic bat - tle of a him and her, I don't like qui - et and I
B7
Em
Am7
D7
1
G
Am7
D7
2
G
Am7
G
wish I were in love a - gain! The
wish I were in love a - gain!
mf
sf

The Lady Is A Tramp

Words by LORENZ HART
Music by RICHARD RODGERS

Moderato
mf
C
Cm7
Dm7
G7
I get too hun - gry for din - ner at eight,
p-mf
C
Cm7
I like the thea - tre but
Dm7
G7
C
Cmaj7
nev - er come late.
I nev - er

C9 F Fm6
both - er with peo - ple I hate,
C C+ F6 G9 C G7
That's why the la - dy is a tramp.
mf
C Cm7 Dm7 G7
I don't like crap - games with Bar - ons and Earls,
C Cm7 Dm7 G7
Won't go to Har - lem in er - mine and pearls.

C Cmaj7 C9 F Fm6
Won't dish the dirt with the rest of the girls,
C C+ F G7 C
Guitar Tacet
That's why the la - dy is a tramp. I like the
Fmaj7 G7 Em7 Am
free fresh wind in my hair,
mf
Dm7 G7 C A7 D7 G7
Life with - out care. I'm broke, it's oke,

C Cm7 Dm E7
Hate Cal - i - for - nia, It's cold and it's damp,
p
Am C+ Am7 1 D7 G7 C Am Dm7 G7
That's why the la - dy is a tramp.
mf
2 D7 D7-5 G7 C Em
la - dy is a tramp.
f
Cm7 Dm Fm G7 C
sf

My Funny Valentine

Words by LORENZ HART
Music by RICHARD RODGERS

Moderately
mp
rit.
p
a tempo
Cm
Be - hold the way our
B♭7
fine - feath-ered friend his
Cm
vir - tue doth pa - rade.
G7
Thou
Cm
know-est not, my
B♭7
dim-wit-ted friend, The
Cm
pic - ture thou hast made,
G
Thy

Cm
Fm
Eb
va- cant brow and thy tous- led hair con - ceal thy good in - tent. Thou
Cm
Eb7
Cm
G7 G7+
no - ble, up - right, truth - ful, sin - cere and slight - ly dop - ey gent, you're
Refrain (slowly, with much expression)
Cm
G7
Cm7
Dm7
My fun - ny Val - en - tine, Sweet com - ic Val - en - tine,
p
Fm
Fm
Fm6 G7
Fm G7
You make me smile with my heart.

Cm G7 Cm7 F7
Your looks are laugh - a - ble, Un - pho - to - graph - a - ble,
Fm Fm7 A♭m B♭7
Yet you're my fav - 'rite work of art. Is your
E♭ B♭7 E♭ B♭7 E♭6 B♭7 E♭ B♭7
fig - ure less than Greek; Is your mouth a lit - tle weak, when you
mf
E♭maj7 G7 Cm A♭maj7 A♭6 A♭7 G7
o - pen it to speak, Are you smart? But

Cm G7 Cm7 F7
don't change a hair for me, Not if you care for me,
p
poco a poco
Fm7 D7♭5 G7 Cm E♭7
Stay, lit-tle Val-en-tine, stay!
cresc.
f molto espress.
A♭ A♭maj7 Fm7 B♭7 1. E♭ A♭7 G7
Each day is Val-en-tine's day.
mf
2. E♭ E♭6
day.
mf
p 8

Where Or When

Words by LORENZ HART
Music by RICHARD RODGERS

In moderate tempo
mp
Cm7 slowly F7 Cm7 F7 B♭7 E♭7
When you're a - wake the things you think come from the dreams you
p
B♭7 E♭7 A♭ Fm7 A♭m6 Fm7 B♭7
dream. Thought has wings, And lots of things are sel-dom what they
E♭6 Cm7 F7 Cm7 F7
seem. Some - times you think you've lived be - fore

All that you live to - day. Things you do come back to you,
As though they knew the way. Oh, the tricks your mind can play!
poco rit.
Refrain (slowly, with very much sentiment)
p
It seems we stood and talked like this be - fore, We
looked at each oth-er in the same way then, But I can't re-mem-ber where or

E♭maj7 E♭6 A♭m6 B♭7 E♭ E♭6
when. The clothes you're wear-ing are the
R.H.
mf
p
E♭maj7 Fm7
clothes you wore. The smile you are smil-ing you were smil-ing then,
E♭maj7 E♭6 Fm6 G7
But I can't re-mem-ber where or when.
Cm Fm7 G7(c) G7 Dm7 G7 Cm
Some things that hap-pen for the first time, Seem to be
mf

Fm7 Cm7 F7 Fm7 B♭7 E♭
hap-pen-ing a - gain. And so it
p
E♭6 E♭maj7 E♭+ Fm
seems that we have met be - fore, and laughed be -
poco a poco
Gm Fm Gm Fm(B♭) Fm B♭7(G) B♭7
fore, and loved be - fore, But who knows where or
cresc. e più espressivo
f
1. E♭ Fm7 E♭maj7 Fm7 B♭7
when!
2. E♭ A♭m6 C♭ E♭
when!
mf
rit.
L.H.
Ped.

Johnny One Note

Words by LORENZ HART
Music by RICHARD RODGERS

Moderately
C
John-ny could on - ly sing one note And the note he sang was
mf
p
Bb C Bb C Bb C C7
this: Ah
mp
F Eb C7 F C7
Poor John - ny One - Note sang out with gus - to And
Poor John - ny One - Note got in A - i - da, In -
p
F C7 F Am Gm7 C7
just o - ver - load - ed the place.
deed a great chance to be brave.

F Eb C7 F C7
Poor John - ny One Note yelled wil - ly - nil - ly, Un -
He took his one note. Howled like the North Wind. Brought
p
F C7 D7 Gm7
til he was blue in the face,
forth wind that made crit - ics rave,
For
While
F Gm7 C7 F
hold - ing one note was his ace.
Ver - di turned round in his grave!
Could - n't hear the
Could - n't hear the
mf
Ab C7 F Am
brass, Could - n't hear the drum, He was in a
flute or the big trom - bone. Ev - 'ry one was

Ab C7 F C7
class By him-self, by gum!
mute, John-ny stood a
F Fm C7 Bbm C7
lone. 8va Cats and dogs stopped yap-ping,
mp
Fm Gm7 C7 Bb C7 Bb C7 Bb6 C7 Bb
Li-ons in the zoo all were jeal-ous of John-ny's big
Fm C7 Fm C7 Bbm C7
trill. Thun-der-claps stopped clap-ping,
mp

Fm Gm7 C7 Bb C7 Bb C7 Bb6 C7
Traf - fic ceased its roar, and they tell us Ni - ag - 'ra stood
Fm C F C
still. He stopped the train - whist - les, Boat - whist - les, Steam - whist - les,
F C7 G#dim C Bb Am C7
Cop - whist - les; All whist - les bowed to his skill.
F Eb C7 F C7
Sing John - ny One - Note sing out with gus - to And
p
F C7 F Am Gm7 C7
just o - ver - whelm all the crowd.

F
E♭
C7
F
C7
Ah!
F
C7
D7
Gm7
So
F
Gm7
C7
F
Gm7
C7
sing, John - ny One Note, out loud!
F
Gm7
C7
F
Gm7
C7
Sing, John - ny One - Note!
F
Gm
C7
F
Sing, John - ny One Note, out loud!
cresc.
e rit.
f marcato

Come And Tell Me

By RICHARD RODGERS and LORENZ HART

Moderately
p
pp
poco rall.
G7sus G7 Cm9 Cm G7sus G7 Cm9 Cm
Guy: I've a most o - blig - ing na - ture do - ing fa - vors is my fun!
Peggy: Sen - ti - men - tal, though the phrase is all you ask of me I'll do.
p a tempo
Bb7sus Bb7 Eb Bb7sus Bb7 Eb Eb+
All you have to do is state your slight - est wish and it is done. You'll
If you tell me, "Go to blaz - es!" I'll trot right a - long for you! No
Ab Eb9+5 Ab Bb7 Eb Bb9+5 Eb
al - ways find me rea - dy and glad to help you out. So
ob - sta - cles sur mount one if help - ful one would be. You
3

Fm C Fm Bb7 Eb Ebdim Bb7sus Bb7 Bb(add9) Bb7
let me be your stea - dy, and shout, "Boy Scout!"
on - ly have to count, "One, two, three" to me!
rall.
Slowly with simple tenderness
Eb Bb7 Eb Bb7
If you want some - one to run down to your par - lor af - ter sun - down,
p-mf a tempo
Eb Ebmaj7 Cm7 F7 Bb7sus Bb7 Bb7sus Bb7 Bb7sus Bb7 Eb
on - ly come and tell me. If you feel you
Bb7 Eb Bb7 Eb Ebmaj7 Cm7 F7
need a ten - der per - son of the oth - er gen - der, on - ly come and

Bb Eb7 Ab Bb7 Eb
tell me. Tell me. If you're blue and sob - by, what a help I'll be;
Eb7 Ab Bb7 Eb Bb7
You can play some hob - by hor - sy on my knee.
Eb Bb7 Eb Eb+ Ab Eb Cm7
If you're op - en to sug - ges - tion on life's most im - por - tant ques - tion, just come and
mf
p
Fm7 Bb7 1 Eb Fm7 Bb+ 2 Eb Ab Fm7 Eb
tell it to me. me.
f
f
8va

This Funny World

By RICHARD RODGERS and LORENZ HART

Moderately Slow
A
mf
p
Very slowly
Edim Em Em(+7) Em Am7 Em
mop! a broom! A pail! The stuff my
Am7 B7 Em Edim Em Em(+7) Em
dreams are made of! You hope; you strive, you

Am D7-5 Gdim G
fail! The world's a place you're not a - fraid of.
Bm Em A7sus A7 Am Em
But soon you are brought down to earth, And you
mf p
Em A7 D7sus D7 Am7/D D7
learn what your dream was worth.
dim. rit.
Very slowly and tenderly
G D7 G
This fun - ny world, makes fun of the things that you strive for.
p

C Fmaj7 F7 G D7 Fm6 E7
This fun-ny world, can laugh at the dreams you're a - live for;
mf
p
Dm E7sus E Am9 Am D7 G Gsus
If you're beat - en con - ceal it! There's no pi - ty for
mf
mp
G Em Em7 F#7 Bm7 E7
you. For the world can - not feel it Just keep to your - self
mf
A7 Dm7 G D7
Weep to your - self This fun - ny world can turn right a - round and for -
p

G C D7 D7-9 G F G7
get you. It's al - ways sure to roll right a - long when you're
mf
cresc.
C C/B C/A C/G A7 Dm7
through. If you are broke you should-n't mind
mf
p
G7 C6 Cm6 G C D7
It's all a joke for you will find This fun - ny world is mak - ing fun of
p
rall.
1 G A7-9 D7 Eb7 D7sus D7
2 G E7-9 D7+5 G
you.
you.
a tempo
mf
p
rall.
mf
pp

Sing For Your Supper

Words by LORENZ HART
Music by RICHARD RODGERS

Moderate and Graceful

mf
p
F C7 F Bb F C F C F C
Hawks and crows do lots of things, But the ca - na - ry on - ly sings.
mp
F C Bb6 C F
She is a cour - te - san on wings, So I've heard.
Cm
Ea - gles and storks are twice as strong, All the ca - na - ry knows is song,

D7
G7
C7sus
C7
But the ca-na-ry gets a-long, Gild-ed bird!
poco rit.
F
Am
F7
Sing for your sup-per and you'll get break-fast, Song-bird al-ways
p-mf a tempo
Dm
F7
B♭
Gm7
C7
eat If their song is sweet to hear.
F
Am
Sing for your lunch-eon And you'll get din-ner,

F7 Dm F7 Bb Bb6 C7
Dine with wine of choice If ro - mance is in your
F6 F Am F F+ Bb6 C7 Gm C7-9
voice. I heard from a wise ca - na - ry,
mf
Fmaj7 Bdim Bb6 C7
Trill - ing makes a fel - low will - ing; So, lit - tle
Gm C7-9 F9 Ab7 Db G7 C7
swal - low, swal - low now. Now is the time to

F Am F7
sing for your sup - per And you'll get break - fast, Song - birds are not
p
Dm F7 Bb Bb6 C7
dumb. They don't buy a crumb of
F7 Bb F F+ Bb6 C7
bread, It's said, So sing and you'll be
1 F Am Dm Am Dm Am Dm C7
fed.
mf
2 F C C7 F
fed.
mf

Falling In Love With Love

Words by LORENZ HART
Music by RICHARD RODGERS

Moderate Waltz
Bb Bbmaj7 Bb6 Bb F7sus
Fall - ing In Love With Love Is fall - ing for make be -
p-mf
F7 Cm7 F7 F7sus F7 F7sus
lieve. Fall - ing In Love With Love Is
F7 Bbmaj7 Bb6 Bbmaj7 Bb6 Bbmaj7
play - ing the fool; Car - ing too
Bb6 Bbmaj7 Bb6 D7sus D7 F6
much is such a ju - ve - nile fan - cy.

D7 Gdim Gm Cm C7 Cm7
Learn - ing to trust is just For chil - dren in school.
cresc.
dim.
F7 Bb Bbmaj7 Bb6
I fell in love with love one
p
Bb F7sus F7 Cm7 F7 F7sus
night When the moon was full,
I was un -
F7 F7sus F7 Bbmaj7 Bb6 Bbmaj7
wise with eyes Un - a - ble to see.

Bb6
Bbmaj7
Bb6
Bbmaj7
Bb6
I fell in love with love, With love ev - er -
D7sus
D7
Gmaj7
G7
Cm
Ddim
last - ing, But love fell
cresc.
Cm7
F7
1 Bb
F7
out with me.
f
2 Bb
Bb6
me.
mf
f

This Can't Be Love

Words by LORENZ HART
Music by RICHARD RODGERS

Moderately
mf
poco rit.
p a tempo
G D7 G D7 G
In Ve - ro-na my late cous-in Ro-me-o Was three times as
D7 G G B7
stu-pid as my Dro - mi - o For he fell in love and then he
Em A9/7 G C♯dim7 Am D7
died of it, Poor half - wit!
poco rit.

Refrain (smoothly)
G6 C7
This can't be love be-cause I feel so well, No
P a tempo
G G6 Am7 D7 Am7 D7 G6
sobs, no sor-rows, no sighs; This can't be
mf
P
C7 G Gdim Am7 D7
love, I get no diz-zy spell. My head is not in the
G C6 C7 G F♯m7 B7
skies. My heart does not stand still, Just hear it
mf

Em
beat!
This is too sweet
B7
to
E7+(♭9)
be
A9
love.
D7(9♭)
D7
This can't be love be-cause I
G6
feel so well; But still I
C7
love to look in your
G6
C♯dim7
Am7
D7
eyes.
G
Am7
D7
1.
eyes.
2.
G
C7
Am7
G
p
mf
mf

Who Are You?

Words by LORENZ HART
Music by RICHARD RODGERS

Moderately
mf
G D7 G7 Em C Cm6
Look in - to the pu - pils of my eyes and you will see what a pret - ty pic - ture
p
G F♯ D7 G D7
luck has sent to me!
Now my life's be - gin - ning as I
G7 Em C Am7 Bm D7 G
bathe in your re - flect - ion Thank you luck, for guid - ing me in the right di - rect - ion!

A7 D9 G6 G
Who are you to give this
p-mf
Dsus D7 Am7 D7 G
world of mine A light and bright - er shine? I won - der
A7 Gsus G7 C
who are you to make a va - cant room
G7 C C D7 G9
A place where flow - ers bloom, And tell me who am
mf

C6 G7 C6 G7
I that when I think of your face I dance in-to
Cm C G7 G+ C6 D7 D7-5 G
space so hap-py and grace-ful too If that's what
A7 D9 G6 G Am7
you can do. I won-der who
D11 1 G 2G C6 G
are you? you?
p
mf espr
mf

Ev'rything I've Got

Words by LORENZ HART
Music by RICHARD RODGERS

Moderately
f
Rhythmically
Eb
Bb9
Bb7
Eb
Don't stamp your foot at me, That's im - po -
p
Bb7
Eb
Cm6
D7
Gm
lite, To stamp your foot at me, Is not quite
Cm6
D7
Gm
Cm
F7
right. All I dis - cov - er is, You're not so
mf

Bb Bb7 Eb Fm7 Bb7 Eb
fine, I fear my lov - er is a swine.
mf p mf
(Brightly)
Eb Bb7 Eb Bb7 Eb Ebm
I have eyes for you to give you dir - ty looks, I have
p-mf mf p
Bb7 Ebm Bb7 Ebm
words that do not come from chil - dren's books, There's a
mf p
F7sus F7 F7sus F7 Bbmaj7 Bb7
trick with a knife, I'm learn - ing to do, And
3
mf

Eb Ab6 Gbm6 Bb7 Eb Bb7
ev - 'ry - thing I've got be - longs to you. I've a
Eb Bb7 Eb Bb7 Eb Ebm
pow'r - ful an - aes - thes - ia in my fist, And the
Bb7 Ebm Bb7 Ebm
per - fect wrist to give your neck a twist,
F7sus F7 F7sus F7
There are ham - mer - lock holds I've mas - tered a

Bbmaj7 Bb7 Eb Ab6 Gm6 Bb7
few, And ev - 'ry - thing I've got be - longs to
mf
Eb Cb Fb Cb Dbm7
you. Share for share, Share a - like,
f
mf
Cb Fb Cb Fb Gb Eb Ab Eb D
You get struck each time I strike, You for me, Me for you,
Gm Bb7 Eb Bb7 Eb Bb7 Eb
I'll give you plen - ty of noth - ing, I'm not yours for bet - ter but for worse,
f
p

Ebm
Bb7
Ebm
Bb7
And I've learned to give the well - known witch - es curse
Ebm
F7sus
F7
F7sus
F7
I've a ter - ri - ble tongue, A tem - per for
Bbmaj7
Bb7
Eb
Ab6
Gm6
Bb7
two, And ev - 'ry - thing I've got be - longs to
1 Eb
Bb7
2 Eb
you. I have you.
mf
p
f
sf

Jupiter Forbid

Words by LORENZ HART
Music by RICHARD RODGERS

Moderately
F C9 F C9 F C9 F C9 F C9
You ought to be proud, tick - led to death go get a breath of this good at - mos -
F6 C9 F6 C9 F C9 F C9 F C9 F C9
phere, You're one of a crowd, all on pa - rade all un - a - fraid and
cresc.
F C9 D7 Gm Adim Gm C7
no one that must fear, Just look a-round and you'll kiss your na - tive

F
ground.
May - be there's a place where peo - ple
May - be there's a place where peo - ple
mp-f
Gm7 C7 F Bb F
nev - er laugh,
nev - er sing,
May - be there's a place where kids don't
Where you have to hide each thing you
mf f p
A Amaj7 A6 C7 F
kid,
did,
May - be there's a place for just the
Where they have a sign "Keep off the
f p
Gm7 C7 F Bb F G#dim C7
up - per half,
Grass" in spring,
Not here
Jup - i - ter for -

1
F
Dm
Gm7
C7
2
F
D
bid.
bid.
Here
f
mf
Em7
A9
Em7
we dance if we see fit,
When he and she fit,
A7
Dmaj7
D6
F6
it's fun.
Bright and
Gm7
C7
Fmaj7
F
Fdim
light as a dan - cer,
For we must an - swer to

C Bb Am C7 F
none. May - be there's a place where you're a -
Gm7 C7 F Bb F
fraid to kiss You could on - ly do it if you
Bm7 E7 Bm7 E7 Am Am6 Am(+7) Am Cm Eb D7
hid, That will nev - er hap - pen in a place like this,
G9 F Guitar Tacet C7 F Gm7 F
Not here. Jup - i - ter for - bid.

Nobody's Heart

Words by LORENZ HART
Music by RICHARD RODGERS

Leisurely
mf
poco rit.
Refrain (slowly, with expression)
F G9 C7 F B♭ F F+ Gm7 C7
No-bod-y's heart be - longs to me, Heigh - ho! Who cares?
p a tempo
F G9 C7 F B♭ F F+ Dm G9 F
No-bod-y writes his songs to me, No___ one be - longs to me, That's the
Gm7 C7 F Fm D♭ B♭7
least of my cares. I may be sad at times, And dis-in-

C G7 C Gm7 C7 Fm D♭ B♭7 C G7(♭5) C
clined to play, But it's not bad at times, To go your own sweet way. —
Gm7 C7 F G7 C7 F B♭ F F+ Dm G9
No-bod-y's arms be - long to me, No ___ arms feel strong to me,
mf
p
F Gm7 C7 Am F6 Gm7 C7 F F+
I ad - mire the moon, As a moon, Just a moon, No-bod-y's heart be-
Bmaj7 B7 C7 1. F Gm7 C7 2. F
Fine
longs to me to - day. day. ___
mf
mf Fine

Trio (much faster)
B♭
Ride Am - a - zon ride.
E♭
mp
F7 Cm7 A♭m6 F7 B♭m B♭ B♭(E♭) B♭
Hunt your stags and bears.
Take life in its stride.
E♭
F7 F7+ B♭maj9 E♭ B♭maj7 B♭6
Heigh - ho! Who cares?
rit.
a tempo

D G
Go hunt - ing with pride,
A9 Em7 Cm6 A7 Dm D D(G) D
Track bears to their lairs.
B♭ Gm6
Ride, Am - a - zon ride!
A7+ A7 D7(♭9) D7 G7+5 G7 C7(♭9) C7
Heigh-ho, Who cares?
Dal 𝄋 al Fine
rit.

Wait Till You See Her

Words by LORENZ HART
Music by RICHARD RODGERS

Moderate waltz tempo
mf
smoothly
p
E♭ E♭m B♭7(♭5) B♭
My friends who knew´ me, Nev - er would know me,
E♭ E♭m B♭7(♭5) B♭ B♭+
They'd look right through me, A - bove and be - low me and
E♭ E♭maj7 Fm7 B♭7
ask "who's that man? Who is that man?

Eb Bb7 Eb Bb7
That's not my light heart-ed friend!" Meet-ing one
Bb+ Eb Bb+ Eb Bb+ Eb Bb7
girl was the start of the end. Love is a
Bb+ Eb Bb+ Eb Bb+ Eb F7 Bb7
sim-ple e-mo-tion a friend should com-pre-
Eb Ebm Eb Eb+
hend.
poco a poco cresc.

Refrain (in spirited tempo)
Fm7 Bb7 Eb Fm7
Wait till you see her, see how she looks, Wait till you
mp
Bb9 Emaj7 Eb6 Fm7 Bb7
hear her laugh. Paint-ers of paint-ings,
Eb Fm7 D7 Gm
writ-ers of books, Nev-er could tell the half.
Cm Cm7 F7 Bb
Wait till you feel the warmth of her glance,
mf

Cm7 G7+(b9) C9(b5) C9 Fm7 Bb7
Pen-sive and sweet and wise. All of it love - ly,
mp
Cm Gm C9 F9 Fm G7
All of it thrill-ing; I'll nev - er be will-ing to free her,
cresc.
f
Ebm F7 E7 Eb7 Fm7 Bb7
When you see her, You won't be - lieve your
rit.
1 Eb
eyes.
a tempo
2 Eb
eyes.
rall.
f
Ped.
*
Ped.
*

Moon Of My Delight

By RICHARD RODGERS and LORENZ HART

Lightly
mf
poco rit.
p a tempo
mp
Db
Gb
Moon of moons, when you are mine Bright the night will be;
You're my moon and I'm your earth, Bless me night with your gaze;
But re - mem - ber, when you shine, Con - cen - trate on
What are love - ly eve - nings worth If I lose your

Db Bb7 Eb7 Ab
me! Moon of moons, be mine a - lone,
rays? If you ev - er should de - part,
Cm7 Ab Bdim Eb7sus Ebm7 Eb7 Ab Bb7 Bdim
Mine a - lone, don't laugh, moon! I could nev - er
I would be a mean cheese; If you leave me,
C7 Fm Gm Fm Eb Bb7 Eb7sus Ebm7 Eb7
care to own A quar - ter or a half moon.
then your heart Must be made of green cheese.
Ab Ab+ Bbm7
Moon of my de - light, I'm going to put a ring a -
p-f

Ebm7
Eb7
Ab
Ab+
round you, You'll stay home to - night!
Bbm7
Ebm7
Eb7
Ab
Scin - till - a - ting where I found you When you were a lit - tle
Gm7
Gm
Eb7
cres - cent, Your man - ners were as soft as wool,
Fm
Bb7
Eb7
Guitar Tacet
Now you're get - ting ef - fer - ves - cent; But, may - be, that's be - cause you're

Eb7
Ab
Ab+
full.
Moon of my de - light,
f
Fm7
Db
C7
F7
If you'd on - ly treat me right,
We could have a sat - el -
Bb7
Ab
Eb7sus
Eb7
lite or two,
Moon of my de -
1
Ab
Fm
Bbm7
Eb7
light!
2
Ab
Bbm7
Db9
Ab
light!
D.S. al Fine
(with repeat)
3
3

My Heart Stood Still

Music by RICHARD RODGERS
Words by LORENZ HART

Moderately
mf espress.
leisurely
F
Eb
He: I laughed at sweet - hearts
She: Through all my school - days
rit.
p a tempo
F
Eb
Db
I met at schools; All in - dis - creet hearts
I hat - ed boys; Those Ap - ril - Fool days

Gm7 C7 F
Seemed ro - man - tic fools. A house in
Brought me love - less joys. I read my
p
A Bm7 E7 C
Ice - land Was my heart's do - main. I
Pla - to, Love, I thought a sin; But
G7 C C7 Am7 Fdim C rit. Gm7 C7
saw your eyes; Now cas-tles rise in Spain!
since your kiss, I'm read-ing Mis - sus Glyn!
rit.
Refrain (slow but liltingly)
F G♯dim Gm7 C7 F F+ Gm7 C7
I took one look at you, That's all I meant to do;
p

F F+ Gm7 C9 F Gm7 C7
And then my heart stood still!
F G♯dim Gm7 C7 F F+ Gm7 C7
My feet could step and walk, My lips could move and talk,
F F+ Gm7 C9 F B♭6 F
And yet my heart stood still! Though not a
Fm C+ C
sin - gle word was spok - en, I could tell you knew,
mp with warm expression

Fm6 G7
That un-felt clasp of hands Told me so
C7+5 C7 Gm7 C+ Gm6 F Am G♯dim Gm7 C7
well you knew. I nev-er lived at all
rall.
p a tempo
F F+ B♭ B♭maj7 Gm7 F C7
Un-til the thrill of that mo-ment when my heart stood
cresc.
dim.
1. F Dm6 Am C7
still.
mf
p
2. F
still.
p smorzando
pp
pp
Ped.

On A Desert Island With Thee

Music by RICHARD RODGERS
Lyric by LORENZ HART

Moderately
mf
rall.
più rall.
C Cdim Dm7 G7 A7 Cm
He: Come, sit thee near; Place thy - self up - on my knee; Make an
p a tempo
G Gdim F G7 C
end of thy fear, For I love but thee in Ca - me - lot.
F♯dim Dm7 G7 C Cm
She: Oh, no not here Where ob - served of all we'll be. Should thy
p grazioso

G Gdim F G7 C
fa - ther ap - pear, He would sure - ly scold and damn a lot.
F C Fm C
He: Care not a jot, Heark-en to my plot:
D7 C D7 G7
Soon we'll re - treat to a sweet spot!
un poco rit.
Refrain (gracefully)
C Dm7 G7 C Fm6
Oh for a year on a des-ert is-land with thee,
p a tempo

C Dm7 G7 C Dm7 G7
Out in the sheer mid-dle of the sea.
mf
C Dm7 G7 C Fm6
We'll sing tra - la; would-n't we be hap-py and gay,
p
C Dm7 G7 C Dm7 G7
With thy mam-ma man-y miles a - way? In the morn-ing air
mp
Dm7 G7 Dm7 G7 Dm7 G7 Dm7 G7
Mur-mur a bless-ing; First we'll eat, Then we will dress. If it's fair,

Dm7 G7 Dm7 G7 D7 G7 C
We'll be ca - ress - ing, If it rains We'll ca - ress! Who knows next
mf
p
Dm7 G7 C Fm6 C
year what the pop - u - la - tion will be; Out in the
Dm7 G7
1. C Dm7 G7
2. C Dm7 G7 C Fine
mid - dle of the sea? sea?
mf
mf
sf Fine
TRIO
C
She: I'll pack each lit - tle thing for thee. What ten books shall I
mf
p

B E B Em G7
bring for thee? (We'll need some books to read;) He: Thou
mp
C B
needst not bring ten books a-long, If thou wilt bring thy looks a-long, 'Twill be e-
p
E G7 C Fm6
nough for me. If the heat be-gins to swel-ter,
mp
Fdim C Fm6
We won't have to fear the sun. We will lie be-neath a shel-ter

Fdim C Em Am6
On - ly big e - nough for one. She: Let the prud-ish peo-ple quar-rel;
Em Am
We'll for-get them for the nonce. If they think our love im - mor- al,
D7 G G7 C
"Hon - i soit qui mal y pense." He: I'll dress the way that A-dam did. She: And I the way his
mp
F C D7 Dm7 G7
Mad-am did. He: I'll see e - nough of thee!
mf
D.S. al Fine
D.S. al Fine

Thou Swell

Music by RICHARD RODGERS
Words by LORENZ HART

Calmly
mf
rit.
In a jolly tempo
B♭7 E♭6 Fm7 B♭9
He: Babe, we are well met, As in a spell met, I lift my hel - met,
She: Thy words are queer, Sir, Un - to mine ear, Sir, Yet thou'rt a dear, Sir,
p
E♭ D7 Fm7 B♭7+ E♭6 B♭dim B♭7
San - dy; You're just dan - dy. For just this
to me; Thou could'st woo me; Now could'st thou
dim.
E♭ E♭6 E♭ B♭7 E♭6
here lad. You're such a fist - full, My eyes are mist - ful,
try, knight. I'd mur - mur "Swell," too, And like it well too;

Fm7 B♭9 E♭ D7 Fm7 B♭+5 E♭6 E♮dim
Are you too wist-ful to care, Do say you care to
More thou wilt tell to San - dy. Thou art dan - dy; Now
B♭7 E♭ E♭6 E♭ Gm Cm
say; "Come near lad." You are so grace - ful,
art thou my knight. Thine arms are mar - tial;
dim.
D7 Gm E♭ Cm D7 Gm
have you wings? You have a face full of nice things;
Thou hast grace; My cheek is par - tial to thy face;
Cm F7 B♭6 Gm Cm7 F7 Fm7 B♭7
You have no speak-ing voice, dear, With ev - 'ry word it sings.
And if thy lips grow wea - ry, Mine are their rest - ing place.
rall.
rit.

Refrain (slowly, with grace)
F9 B♭7 F9 B♭7 F9 B♭7 F9 B♭7
Thou swell! Thou wit-ty! Thou sweet! Thou grand! Wouldst
mp
E♭6 B♭9 E♭6 B♭9 E♭6 B♭9 E♭ Adim B♭7 C
kiss me pret-ty? Wouldst hold my hand? Both thine eyes are cute too;
mf
Fm B♭ E♭ E♭6 E♭ E♭+5 A♭6 G7
What they do to me. Hear me hol-ler I choose a Sweet
dim.
mf
mp
Cm7 F B♭7 B♭+ Fm F9 B♭7 F9
lol-la - pa-loo-sa in thee. I'd feel so
mf
mp

Bb7 F9 Bb7 F9 Bb7 Eb6 Bb9 Eb6 Bb9
rich in a hut for two; Two rooms and kit-chen I'm
Eb6 Bb9 Eb6 Ebdim Bb7 C Fm Bb
sure would do; Give me just a plot of, Not a lot of
mf
G7 C+7 C7 F7 Bb7
land, And Thou swell! Thou wit-ty! Thou
1. Eb F#dim Bb7 F9 2. Eb Bb7 Eb6 Bb7 Eb
grand! Thou grand!
mf
mf
sf

To Keep My Love Alive

Music by RICHARD RODGERS
Lyric by LORENZ HART

Moderately
mf
p
A7 D G7 (sus C) G7 C A7
I've been mar-ried and mar-ried, and of-ten I've sighed,
D Gm7 C7 Gm7 F Em7
I'm nev-er a brides-maid, I'm al-ways the bride;
A7 D G7 (sus C) G7 C A7
I never di-vorced them, I had-n't the heart,

D Dm E7 D E7 A7 (sus D) A7
Yet, re-mem-ber these sweet words, "Till death do us part."
rit.
Refrain (with care and elegance)
D D6 Dmaj7
I mar-ried man-y men, a ton of them, be-cause I was un-true to
I thought Sir George had pos-si-bil-i-ties, but his flir-ta-tions made me
p a tempo
D Em A7 D D+
none of them, be-cause I bumped off ev-'ry one of them to
ill at ease, and when I'm ill at ease, I kill at ease to
Em A7 D D
keep my love a-live. Sir Paul was frail, he looked a
keep my love a-live. Sir Charles came from a san-a-

D6 Dmaj7 D
wreck to me. At night he was a hor-se's neck to me, so
to-ri-um, and yelled for drinks in my em - po-ri-um. I
Em A7 D D+ Em A7 D
I per-formed an ap-pen-dec-to-my, to keep my love a-live! Sir
mixed one drink, he's in me-mo-ri-am, to keep my love a-live! Sir
mf
Gm7 C7 F Gm7 C7 F
Tho-mas had in-som-ni-a, he could-n't sleep at night, I
Fran-cis was a sing-ing bird, a night-in-gale, That's why I
A7 D E7 (sus A) E7 A7
bought a lit-tle ar-sen-ic, he's sleep-ing now all right. Sir
tossed him off my bal-co-ny to see if he could fly Sir

D D6 Dmaj7
Phil-ip played the harp, I cussed the thing. I crowned him with his harp to
Ath-el-stane in-dulged in frat-ri-cide, he killed his dad and that was
D Em A7 D D+
bust the thing, and now he plays where harps are just the thing, to
pat-ri-cide. One night I stabbed him by my mat-tress side, to
Em A7 D+ 1. G C A7(♭5) D
ten. ten.
keep my love a-live, to keep my love a-live.
keep my love a-live, to
ten. ten.
ten ten
a tempo
A7 2. G C A7(♭5) D
ten. ten.
I keep my love a-live.
ten. ten.
sf

Can't You Do A Friend A Favor?

By RICHARD RODGERS and LORENZ HART

Moderately
mf
mp
Eb
Bb7
Fm7
Bb7
Fm7
Bb7
Fm
Bb7
Fm
Bb7
Fm7
Bb7
Ab
Eb
Cm6
mf
You can count your friends on the fin - gers of your hand, If you're luck - y you have
two, I have just two friends, that is all that I de - mand, on - ly two, Just me and
you. And a good friend heeds a friend, when a good friend needs a

Fm7 Bb7 G7 Cm F9 Fm7 Bb7
friend. Can't you do a friend a fa - vor?
p-mf
G7 Cm F9 Fm7 Bb7
Can't you fall in love with me?
Fm6 G7 Cm F9 Cm7
Life a - lone can lose its fla - vor
Ebdim Fm7 Bb7 Ebmaj7 Eb6
You could make it sweet, you see!

Dm7 G7 Cm F9 Fm7 Bb7 G7
I'm the dish you ought to sa - vor
Cm F9 Bb7 D Bb7 Eb
Some - thing warm and some - thing new;
I could do my
C7+5(b9) C7 Fm7 F9 Eb Fm7 Bb7
friend a fa - vor,
I could fall in love with
mp mf p
Eb Dm7 G7 Eb
you.
you.
mf f mf

Bye And Bye

Words by LORENZ HART
Music by RICHARD RODGERS

Moderately Fast
p
poco rall.
a tempo
F C/E Dm7 Fmaj7 Gm7 C7 F C/E
If you'll on - ly bide the time And for - ti - fy your heart, For - tune will de -
Why should we be sor - row - ful When just a - head we see Pic - tures of to -
Dm7 Fmaj7 Bb Gm7 C7 Cm7 F9 Bb
cide the time When sor - rows will de - part. Let's put heads to - geth - er
mor - row full, Of things that ought to be? We won't know a trou - ble;
poco a poco cresc.
Cm7 F7sus F7 Bb Gm7 C9 Dm7 Gm7
And be fan - cy free. Make your trou - bles dis - ap - pear, Let bliss ap - pear And
We won't know a care; Ev' - ry storm we weath - er, dear, To - geth - er, dear, Seems

Bdim
F/C
Dm
Gm7
G7
C11
C7
see all the jol - ly times of days to be.
fair While we dream of all we'll have to share.
mf
p poco rall.
mf
mp
F
F6
Fmaj7
Bye and bye Not now but bye and bye Some - how we'll try and buy
p-f a tempo
F6
Gm7
C7
Gm7
C
Gm
A lit - tle nest. Scheme a - while when lone - ly,
C7
F
Dream a - while 'Twill on - ly seem a - while And love will do the rest.

C7 F F6
Our hap - py days will come Though slight de - lays will come The bright sun's
p
F F13 Bb Gm7
rays will come From out the sky. Ev' - ry cloud
cresc.
mf
Bdim F/C C#dim Dm Bbm6 Fmaj7 Dm Gm7 C7
just flies on, Love is on the far hor - i - zon, You'll be my sweet - heart Bye and
poco rit.
1 F C7
bye.
p a tempo
mf
2 F6
bye.
Ped.

Here In My Arms

Music by RICHARD RODGERS
Lyric by LORENZ HART

Moderately and leisurely
F Bb F Dm
I know a mer-ry place
I know a pret-ty place
mf
p dolce
Bb6 C7 F Bb6 F Bb F Dm Bb6 C7
Far from in-tru-sion. It's just the ver-y place For your se-
At your com-mand, sir; It's not a cit-y place, Yet near at
F Am Ab Bbm7 Eb7 Ab Fm
clu-sion. There you can while a-way Days as you
hand, sir; Here, if you loll a-way, Two hearts can
mp

B♭m6 C7 F E♭ F Dm Gm C7 F B♭ C7
smile a - way, It's not a mile a - way But it's new to you.
toll a - way. You'd nev - er stroll a - way, If you on - ly knew!
p
poco rall.
Refrain (tenderly)
F B♭m F6
Here in my arms it's a - dor - a - ble! It's de -
p a tempo
C7 F B♭6 F B♭ F
plor - a - ble That you were nev - er there. When lit - tle
B♭m F6 C7
lips are so kiss - a - ble It's per - mis - si - ble

F Bb6 F Bb Gb7
— For me to ask my share — Next to my heart it is
mf cresc.
Bb F Fmaj7 Dm7 G7 Gm7
ev-er so lone-ly, I'm hold-ing on-ly air,
C7+5 F Bbm F
While here in my arms it's a-dor-a-ble! — It's de-
p
C7 F Bb6 1.F C7 2.F
plor-a-ble — That you were nev-er there. — there. —
mf
sf
Ped.

College On Broadway

Music by RICHARD C. RODGERS
Lyric by LORENZ M. HART

March Tempo
f
sfz
C
A7-5
Dm7
G7
On high O - lym-pus, might - y Jove all pow - er - ful
p
C
Am7
D7
G
Once asked Min - er - va, "Where's your ho - ly shrine on earth?" A -
GmGdim
Gm
Gm(+5)
Gm6A7/G
Cm7
F7
pol - lo, Mars, and Mer - cu - ry cried "Dad, With

G/B Gdim Am7 D7 G A9 G7
Min - nie, dear, the same old shrine we've had:"
C Dm7 G7 Dm7 G7
Bull - dogs run a - round New Ha - ven;
p-f
C Dm7 G7 Dm7 G7 Dm7
Har - vard paints old Cam - bridge red; E - ven
Em7 Asus Am Am(+7) Am7 D6
poor old Phil - a - del - phia real - ly has a col - lege

Dm7 G+ C Dm7 G7
it is said; And Wil - liams - town be - longs to Wil -
Dm7 G7 Am C7 F
liams; Prince - ton's ti - ger stands at bay, But
D7 C/G A A7 Dm
old New York won't let the world for - get that there's a
Dm7 G7 1 C 2 C
Guitar Tacet
col - lege on Broad - way. way.
sfz

Dancing On The Ceiling

(He Dances On My Ceiling)

Music by RICHARD RODGERS
Lyric by LORENZ HART

Moderately
mf
poco rit.
p a tempo
F
The world is lyr - i - cal
Ddim7
Be - cause a mir - a - cle
Gm7
Has brought my lov - er to
C7
F
me!
Fm
Though he's some oth - er
F
C7-5
place,
C7
His

C7+ C7 F
face I see. At night I creep in bed
Ddim7 Gm7 C7 F
And nev - er sleep in bed, But look a - bove in the air.
Fm F C7-5 C7 C7+ C7 F
And to my great - est joy, my boy is there!
Am D9 Gm C9
It is my prince who walks in - to my dreams and talks.
rallent.
poco rit.
Ped.
Ped.

Refrain (liltingly)
p-mf
F F+ Gm G7 C Em
He danc-es o-ver-head on the ceil-ing, near my bed,
Gm7 C7 F Gm C7 F
In my sight, Through the night.
F F+ Gm G7 C Em
I try to hide in vain Un-der-neath my coun-ter-pane;
Gm7 C7 F Gm C7 F
There's my love up a-bove!

C7
F
I whis-per "Go a-way, my lov-er, It's not fair,"
mp
C7
F Cdim7 C7
But I'm so grate-ful to dis-cov-er He's still there.
F F+ Gm G7 C Em Gm7
I love my ceil-ing more Since it is a danc-ing floor Just for
p
C7
1. F Gm7 C7
2. F
my love. love.
mf
Ped.

Manhattan

(From the Broadway Musical "GARRICK GAITIES")

Lyric by LORENZ HART
Music by RICHARD RODGERS

Brightly
mf
F Bb Bbm F Bb Bbm F
Sum-mer jour-neys to Ni-ag-'ra, And to oth-er plac-es ag-gra-vate all our
p
Fmaj7 Gm7 C7 F6 F Bb Bbm
cares; We'll save our fares; I've a co-zy lit-tle flat in
F Bb Bbm F F9 D7 Gm Bbm6 C7
what is known as old Man-hat-tan, We'll set-tle down right here in town.

Refrain (gaily, but not fast)
F Fdim Gm7 C7 Fmaj7
We'll have Man-hat - tan, The Bronx and Stat - en Is - land too; ___
We'll go to Green-wich Where mod - ern men itch To be free; ___
We'll go to Yonk-ers Where true love con-quers In the wilds; ___
We'll have Man-hat - tan The Bronx and Stat - en Is - land too; ___
mp
F6 Fdim Gm7 C7 C+ F Gm7 C7
___ It's love - ly go - ing through ___ the Zoo; ___
___ And Bowl-ing Green you'll see ___ with me; ___
___ And starve to - geth - er, dear ___ in Childs' ___
___ We'll try to cross Fifth Av - - en - ue; ___
F Fdim Gm7 C7 Edim Dm
It's ver - y fan - cy On old De - lan - cey Street, you know; ___
We'll bathe at Bright - on, The fish you'll fright - en When you're in; ___
We'll go to Cone - y And eat bo - logn - y on a roll; ___
As black as on - yx We'll find the Bron - nix Park Ex - press; ___

A Fm G7 Dm7 Fm G7 Gm7 C7
The sub-way charms us so, When balm-y breez-es blow
Your bath-ing suit so thin Will make the shell-fish grin
In Cen-tral Park, we'll stroll Where our first kiss we stole,
Our Flat-bush flat I guess Will be a great suc-cess.
mf
F Fdim Gm7 C7
To and fro; And tell me what street com-pares with Mott Street
Fin to fin; I'd like to take a sail on Ja-mai-ca
Soul to soul; Our fu-ture ba-bies we'll take to A-bie's
More or less; A short va-ca-tion On In-spir-a-tion
mp
Fmaj7 F6 Fdim Gm7 C7 C+
in Ju-ly, Sweet push carts gently glid-ing
Bay with you; And fair Can-ar-sie's Lake we'll
I-rish Rose, I hope they'll live to see it
Point we'll spend And in the sta-tion house we'll

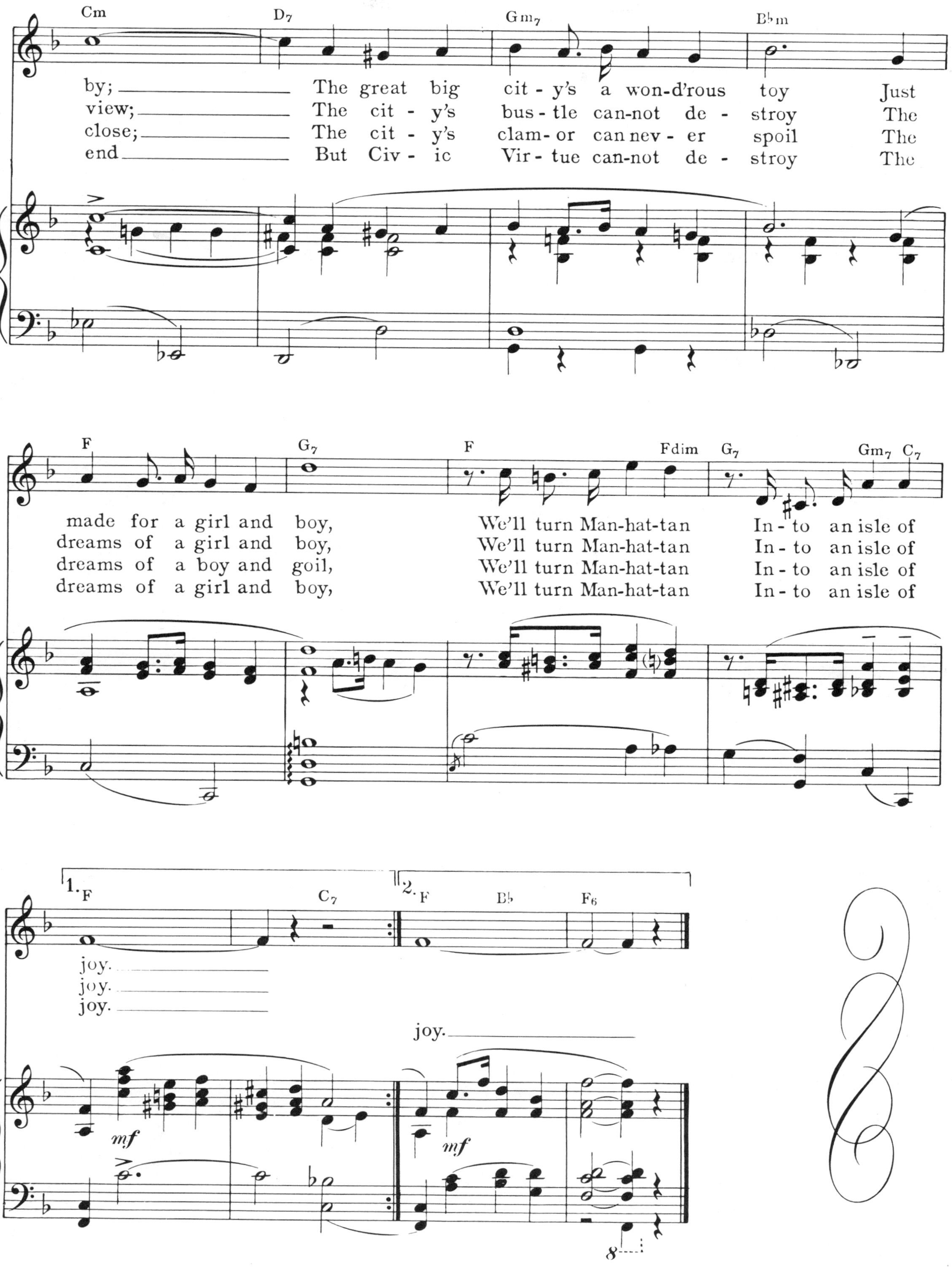
Cm D7 Gm7 B♭m
by; The great big cit - y's a won-d'rous toy Just
view; The cit - y's bus - tle can-not de - stroy The
close; The cit - y's clam - or can nev - er spoil The
end But Civ - ic Vir - tue can-not de - stroy The
F G7 F Fdim G7 Gm7 C7
made for a girl and boy, We'll turn Man-hat-tan In - to an isle of
dreams of a girl and boy, We'll turn Man-hat-tan In - to an isle of
dreams of a boy and goil, We'll turn Man-hat-tan In - to an isle of
dreams of a girl and boy, We'll turn Man-hat-tan In - to an isle of
1. F C7
2. F B♭ F6
joy.
joy.
joy.
joy.
mf
mf
8

Sentimental Me

Words by LORENZ HART
Music by RICHARD RODGERS

Lightly
mf
cresc.
rit.
C
Gdim
G7
Cdim
C
Look at me a - gain, dear; Let's hold hands and then, dear, Sigh in
Dar-ling you're so hand-some, Strong and clev - er and some-times you
p a tempo
D7
G7
C
cho - rus; It won't bore us, to be sure;
seem, dear, Like a dream, dear, that came true.
mf

C Gdim G7 Cdim C
There's no mean - ing to it, Yet we o - ver - do it, With a
That's why I picked you out; Bet - ter men I threw out Of my
p
D7 G7 C Ab C Ab
rel - ish that is hell - ish to en - dure;
liv - ing room while giv - ing room to you;
mf
F G7 C
I am not the kind that mere - ly flirts;
I would rath - er read of love in books;
marcato
D7 Dm G7
I just love and love un - til it hurts.
Love is much more pain - ful than it looks.

Refrain (gracefully)
C+7 F G7 G+7 C C+
Oh, sen-ti-men-tal me and poor ro - man-tic you;
mp
F G7 G+7 C G7 C Dm7 Fm6
Dream-ing dreams is all that we can do; We hang a - round all day and
mp
Dm7 G7 G+7 C Gm A7 A7(♭5) G Ddim
pon-der, While both of us grow fond - er The Lord knows where we're
D7 Dm7 G7 C7+ F G7 G+7
wan-der - ing to! I sit and sigh; you sigh and sit up -
mf
mp

C C+ F G7 G+7
on my knee; We laugh and cry, and nev-er dis-a-
C G7 C Dm7 Fm6 Dm7 G7 G+7
gree; A mil-lion kiss-es we'll make theft of Un-
C G+ C E7 Am Dm7 C G+7
til there's noth-ing left of Poor ro-man-tic you and sen-ti-men-tal
1. 2.
C C7 F C+7 C Fm7 C
me. Oh, me.
f

Mountain Greenery

Music by RICHARD RODGERS
Lyric by LORENZ HART

Moderately
mf
rall.
p a tempo
grazioso
C C+ F6 B♭ G7 C
On the first of May It is mov - ing day;
Sim - ple cook - ing means More than French cui - sines.
Em Em7 Am F D7 G G+ C Am6 Adim
Spring is here, so blow your job, Throw your job a - way;
I've a ban - quet planned which is sand - wich - es and beans,
G G+ C F D7 G7
Now's the time to trust To your wan - der - lust.
Cof - fee's just as grand With a lit - tle sand.
poco a poco cresc.

E7
Am
G
G7
In the cit - y's dust you wait, Must you wait? Just you wait:
Eat and you'll grow fat - ter, boy, S'mat - ter, boy? 'At - ta boy!
un poco rit.
Refrain (Cheerfully)
C Am Dm7 G7 C Am Dm7 G7
In a moun-tain green - er - y, Where God paints the scen - er - y,
In a moun-tain green - er - y, Where God paints the scen - er - y,
p-f a tempo
C F D7 G Am7 Gdim G
Just two craz - y peo - ple to - geth - er;
Just two craz - y peo - ple to - geth - er;
C Am Dm7 G7 C Am Dm7 G7
While you love your lov - er, let Blue skies be your cov - er-let,
How we love se - ques - ter-ing Where no pests are pest - er-ing,

C F D7 G C Gdim G C7+5
When it rains we'll laugh at the weath - er And if you're good
No dear ma - ma holds us in teth - er! Mos - qui - toes here
cresc.
F6 C7 F6 Fm6
I'll search for wood, So you can cook
Won't bite you, dear; I'll let them sting
Em7 D7 Dm7 G7
While I stand look - - - ing.
Me on the fing - - - er.
C Am Dm7 G7 C Am Dm7 G7
Beans could get no keen - er re - cep - tion in a bean - er - y,
We could find no clean - er re - treat from life's ma - chin - er - y
mp

C Am Dm7 G7
Bless our moun-tain green-er-y home!
Than our moun-tain green-er-y
1. C Dm7 G7
2. C
home!
3. C Trio–Patter
home!
mf
f-p
C G7 C
He: When the world was young, Old Fa-ther Ad-am with sin would
p
sempre staccato
C G7
grap-ple, So we're en-tit-led to just one ap-ple, I mean to

C
C
make ap - ple sauce. ___
She: Un - - der-neath the
(over L.H.)
mf
p
G7
C
bough ___ We'll learn a les - son from Mis - ter O - mar; ___ Be-neath the
stacc.
G7
C
eyes of no Pa and no Ma ___ Old La - dy Na - ture is boss. ___
Em
A7
___
He: Wash-ing dish - es, Catch - ing fish - es
(over L.H.)
mf
mp

Am Em B7 Em A7
In the run-ning stream, We'll curse the smell o' Cit - ron-el-la
Am7 D7 G7 C G7
E - ven when we dream. She: Head upon the ground Your down-y
mf
mp
stacc.
C G7
pil - low is just a bould - er. He: I'll have new dim-ples be - fore I'm
C C+ C C7+5 F
old - er; But life is peach-es and cream. And if you're good,

C7 F Fm6 Em7
I'll search for wood, So you can cook.
D7 Dm7 G7 C Am
While I stand look - - - ing. Beans could
mp
Dm7 G7 C Am Dm7 G7 C Am
get no keen - er re - cep - tion in a bean - er - y. Bless our
Dm7 G7 C
moun-tain green - er - y home.
f
Ped.

The Girl Friend

Music by RICHARD RODGERS
Lyric by LORENZ HART

Joyously
mf
rit.
C
p a tempo
He: My girl's the kind of girl for stead - y com - pa - ny. It's stead - y com - pa - ny That I pre - fer. When in the Charles - ton dance I want to bump a knee, I want to
She: He's ver - y short on looks but long on de - cen - cy, He's long on de - cen - cy, He's ver - y tame. But he has made an aw - ful hit with me since he, A hit with

G7 C E C♯7
bump a knee with her. Home - - ly
me since he first came. I have
espressivo
F♯m B7 E C♯7 F♯m B7 E C♯7
wrecks ap-peal When their checks ap-peal, But she has
seen so well, He won't screen so well, But that boy
F♯m B7 E G7
sex - ap-peal, Yes, sir!
means so well, He's game!
mf
Refrain (a little faster and rhythmical)
C C♯dim G7 Cdim
He: Is - n't she cute! Is - n't she sweet! She's
She: Is - n't he cute! Is - n't he sweet! He's
mf

C E7 Fmaj7 Dm7
gen - tle and men - tal - ly near - ly com - plete. She's
gen - tle and men - tal - ly near - ly com - plete. It's
C C#dim G7
knock - out, she's re - gal, her beau - ty's il - le - gal, She's the
strange that this goil can a - dore such an oil - can, I'm the
C Am F6 A♭+ G7 C C#dim
girl friend!
girl friend!
Take her to dance,
He: Take her to dance,
f
p
G9 Cdim C E7
take her to tea! It's stun - ning how cun - ning this
take her to tea! It's stun - ning how cun - ning this

Fmaj7 Dm7 C C♯dim
la - dy can be. A look at this vi - sion will
la - dy can be. She ain't got no cul - ture, she's
G7 C Am F6 A♭+ G7 C
cause a col - li - sion, She's the girl friend!
keen as a vul - ture, She's the girl friend!
Em B7 Em B7
She is smart, She's re - fined, How can she be
She: He is smart, He's re - fined, How can he be
mf
Em G7 C G7 sus4 G7
real? She has heart, She has mind,
real? He has heart, He has mind,

C C♯dim G7 C C♯dim
Hell, the girl's I - deal! Is - n't she cute,
Hell, the boy's I - deal! He: Is - n't she cute,
p
G7 Cdim C E7 Fmaj7 Dm7
Is - n't she sweet? An eye - ful you'd die full of pleas - ure to meet. In
Is - n't she sweet? An eye - ful you'd die full of pleas - ure to meet. Both: In
C C♯dim G7
my fun - ny fash - ion I'm cursed with a pas - sion For the
my fun - ny fash - ion I'm cursed with a pas - sion For the
1. C Am Fm6 G7
girl friend!
{girl boy} friend!
mf
2. C D7(♭5) C G7 C
girl friend!
{girl boy} friend!
f

Blue Room

Music by RICHARD RODGERS
Lyric by LORENZ HART

Moderately
mf
p
not fast
Fmaj7 Bb Fmaj7 Bb Fmaj7
He: All my fu - ture plans, Dear, will suit your plans, Read the lit - tle
She: From all vis - i - tors And in - quis - i - tors, We'll keep our a -
p
Bb F Bb F Fmaj7 Bb Fmaj7
blue prints; Here's your moth - er's room, Here's your
part - ment; I won't change your plans, You ar -
8va
mf
p
Bb Fmaj7 Bb F Bb F
broth - er's room, On the wall are two prints.
range your plans Just the way your heart meant;
8va
mf

D7 Gm D7 Gm D7
Here's the kid - dies' room, Here's the bid - dy's room, Here's a pan - try
Here, we'll be our - selves And we'll see our - selves Do - ing all the
mp
Gm7 C7 F6 C7 Fmaj7 B♭ Fmaj7
lined with shelves, dear, Here I've planned for us, Some - thing
things we're schem - ing, Here's a cer - tain place, Cre - tonne
B♭ Fmaj7 B♭ B♭maj7 Gm7 C7
rall.
grand for us, Where we two can be our - selves, dear;
cur - tain place, Where no one can see us dream - ing:
rall.
Refrain (slowly, with expression)
F C7 F C7
We'll have a blue room, A new room, For two room, Where
p dolce

F F7 Bb Gm7 F G7
ev - 'ry day's a hol - i - day Be - cause you're mar-ried to
mf
Gm7 C7 F C7 F
me. Not like a ball - room A small room, A
p
C7 F F7 Bb
hall room, Where {I / you} can smoke {my / your} pipe a - way, With
mf
F Bb C7 F C7
{your / my} wee head up - on {my / your} knee. We will thrive on, keep a - live on
R. H.

F C7 Gm7 C7
Just noth-ing but kiss - es, With Mis-ter and Mis - sus
mf
Dm7 G7 Gm7 C7 F C7
On lit-tle blue chairs.
You sew your trous-seau, And
I'll wear my
p
F C7 F F7 B♭ Gm7
Rob-in - son Cru-soe is not so far from world-ly cares As our
mf
F Gm7 C7 1.F Gm7 C7 2.F
blue room far a-way up-stairs! stairs!
poco rall.
mf

I Gotta Get Back To New York

By RICHARD RODGERS and LORENZ HART

Moderately, in 2
mf
C F C F C F C F C F C F
Way up north the sun 'll al - ways shine, That love - ly Hud - son
C F C F Dm/C G7 C
Guitar Tacet
Tun - nel is my Ma - son Dix - on Line.
Eb Ab Eb Ab Eb Ab Eb Ab Eb Ab Eb Ab
Where the tem - po rac - es, let me be, Those great wide o - pen

Eb Ab Eb Ab Fm/Eb Bb7 Eb6 Eb Eb6 Eb
spac - es are plac - es that smoth - er me.
B E B E B Bb+ D G D G D A/G
If I'm in Mi - am - i, Bu - da - pest or Rome, I'll al - ways shout, "O.
D/F# E7 A7 C/D D7 E7/G#
Moderately slow, in 4
Am7 D7
K. New York, the prod - i - gal goes home." I'll climb up that Wool - worth and
Ritard.
a tempo
Gmaj7 Em7 Am7 D7 Gmaj7 Em9
kiss ev' - ry floor, The sub - way makes mu - sic for me with a roar, I'm

A9 Am7-5 F#/A# Bm7 E7sus E7 Am7 D7 D+ Gmaj9 G6 Gmaj7 E7/G#
dy-ing to feel that I'm liv-ing once more, I've got-ta get back to New York. There's
Am7 D7 Gmaj7 Em7 Am7 D7
on-ly one stat-ue, I know you'll a-gree, That dame with the torch look-ing
Gmaj9 Em9 A9 Am7-5 F#/A# Bm7 E7sus E7
o-ver the sea, The smell of the Bronx is per-fume to me, I've
Dm7 D7 G Gmaj7 G7+5 C G
got-ta get back to New York. Train, keep on go-ing. Train,

C G B7 Em
I'm riding home again. Feet, keep on stepping. Feet,
F9 E9 Am7 D7 E7/G♯ Am7 D7 Gmaj7 Em7
I'll never say retreat. New York is New York, that's all you can say, It
f
poco rit.
mf a tempo
Am7 D7 Gmaj9 Em9 A9 Am7-5 F♯/A♯
gets in your blood and it's in there to stay. I'm one of six million who
Bm7 E7sus E7 Am7 D7 1 G Am E7/G♯ 2 G G(add 9)
can't keep away, I've got-ta get back to New York. I'll York.
f

You Are Too Beautiful

By RICHARD RODGERS and LORENZ HART

Moderately
mp
freely
Cmaj7 F6 Am7 Dm7 C Cmaj7
Like all fools, I be - lieved what I want - ed to be - lieve,
mp
Dm7 G7 Cmaj7 F6 Am7 Dm7
My fool - ish heart con - ceived what fool - ish hearts con -
C F C Bm7 E7(♭5) Am7
ceive. I thought I found a mir - a - cle, I

Cmaj9 C9 F+ Dm Cmaj7 G9
thought that you'd a - dore me, But it was not a
C6 Am7 D7(b5) Fmaj7 G9
mir - a - cle, It was mere - ly a mi - rage be - fore me.
rit.
Refrain (with expression and not fast)
Dm7 G7 Em7 A7+ Dm7 G7+
You are too beau - ti - ful, my dear, to be true, And I am a fool for
mp
Cmaj7 Em7 Eb7 Dm7 Fm6 G9 C6 Cmaj7 Cdim
beau - ty. Fooled by a feel - ing that be - cause I had found you,
3

Dm7 G7 Em7 C A7(♭9) Dm7 G7
I could have bound you, too. You are too beau - ti - ful for
Em7 A7+ Dm7 G7+ Cmaj7 Em7 E♭7
one man a - lone, For one luck - y fool to be with,
Dm7 Fm6 G9 C6 Ddim Am7 D7 D7+ Dm7 G7(♭9)
When there are oth - er men with eyes of their own to see
C Dm7 C F Cdim C Em6 Gdim Dm7 G7
with. Love does not stand shar - ing, Not if one
p

Cmaj9 C6 Dm6 E7 Am C+ Am7 D7
cares. Have you been com - par-ing My ev-'ry kiss with
Dm7 G7 Dm7 G7 Em7 A7+
theirs? If on the oth-er hand, I'm faith-ful to you, It's
mp
Dm7 G7+ Cmaj7 Em7 Eb7 Dm7 Fm6 G9
not through a sense of du-ty; You are too beau-ti-ful and
C6 Ddim Am7 D7 D7+ Dm7 G7(b9) 1. C Fmaj7 Cmaj7 Ab9 2. C6 Bb6 C(6+9)
I am a fool for beau - ty. ty.
p

A Ship Without A Sail

Music by RICHARD RODGERS
Lyric by LORENZ HART

Moderately slow tempo
mf poco a poco cresc.
rall.
E♭ Fm E♭ B♭9
He: I don't know what day it is, Or if it's dark or fair; Some-
She: When love leaves you all a - lone, You're liv - ing in the past;
molto legato
mp a tempo
Cm F7 Fm7 B♭7
how, that's just the way it is, And I don't real - ly
Then you feel so small a - lone, And oh! the world seems
mf

E♭ E♭ Fm
care. I go to this or that place, I
vast. You tell your grief to no girls, You
mp
E♭ E♭9 Cm F7
seem a - live and well; My head is just a hat place, My
nev - er make it known; Your smile is like a show-girl's, Your
A♭6 G7 A♭ (B♭) Fm
breast an emp - ty shell! And I've a
laugh a hol - low tone. And then your
E♭ E♭+ A♭ B♭7 E♭
fad - ed dream to sell.
lit - tle heart's a stone.
mf

Refrain (not fast)
E♭7 A♭ B♭7 E♭ E♭7 A♭ B♭7 E♭
All a - lone, all at sea! Why does no-bod - y care for me,
p
A♭ G7 Cm A♭m E♭ B♭m6 C7
When there's no love to hold _ my love? Why is my heart so frail,
Fm B♭7 E♭ B♭7
Like a ship with - out a sail? Out on the o - cean,
mp
E♭ B♭7 Fm B♭7
sail-ors can use a chart; I'm on the o - cean guid-ed by just a

E♭ G7 E♭7 A♭ B♭7 E♭
lone - ly heart. Still a - lone, still at sea!
E♭7 A♭ B♭7 E♭ A♭ G7 Cm7 A♭m
Still there's no one to care for me When there's no hand to hold_ my hand.
E♭ B♭m6 C7 Fm7 B♭7
Life is a love - less tale For a ship with - out a
1.E♭ E♭dim E♭ A9 2.E♭
sail. sail.
f
poco rit.
p

Disgustingly Rich

Words by LORENZ HART
Music by RICHARD RODGERS

Moderately
mf
Eb
Bb7
Eb
Bb7
Eb
Bb7
Eb
Bb7
Hilda: Bren - da Fraz - ier sat on a wall. Bren - da Fraz - ier had a big fall.
Eb
Bb/D
Cm
Gm/Bb
Fm/Ab
Fm
Eb/Bb
Eb/G
Bb7
All: Bren - da Fraz-ier's fall-ing down, fall-ing down, fall-ing down. Bren - da Fraz-ier's
Fairly Bright
Eb/Bb
Ab6
Bb7
Eb
Ab/Bb
Eb/Bb
Lacky:
fall-ing down, my fair Min-nie!
f

Bb7
Ab/Bb
Bb7
Eb6
Eb
Sandy: There's mon-ey in the mov - ies, There's
mf
Bb9
Ebmaj7
mon - ey in the ads. There's mon-ey in the old Johns,
Fm7
There's mon - ey in the lads.
Gm7
Guitar Tacet
Abmaj7
Guitar Tacet
G7
Min - nie, Min - nie, Min - nie, Min - nie, Mon - ey, Mon - ey, Mon - ey, Mon - ey, Een - y, Meen - y Mon - ey

Cm
Eb7/Bb
Ab
C7/G
Fm
Guitar Tacet
Fm7
Bb7
Mo. Catch a for - tune by the toe!
ritard.
Moderately
Fm7
Bb7
Eb
Bb7
Eb
Fm7
(Sandy) I'll buy ev' - ry - thing I wear at Sacks,
Boy: Break my an - kles on the ten - nis courts,
mf
Eb/G
Ab
Gm/Bb
Ab/C
Bb7
I'll cheat plen - ty on my in - come tax,
Get pneu - mo - nia do - ing win - ter sports.
Swear like a troup-er,
Hilde: I won't be civ - il,
Eb
Fm7
Guitar Tacet
Fm/Bb
F+/B
Bb7
live in a stu - por, Just dis - gust - ing-ly rich!
rude as the div - il, Just dis - gust - ing-ly rich!

Eb Bb7 Eb Fm7 Eb/G Ab
I'll make mon-ey and I'll make it quick, Boost-ing cig-a-rettes that
Byng: Ev'-ry week-end I will sail the sea On my lit-tle yacht, the
Gm/Bb Ab/C Bb7 Eb
make me sick. Smoth-ered in sa-bles like Bet-ty Gra-ble's
Nor-man-die. Sandy: Catch bar-ra-cu-da down in Ber-mu-da,
Fm7 Guitar Tacet Ab/Bb Eb Fm7 Eb7/G Ab
Just dis-gust-ing-ly rich! I will buy land
Just dis-gust-ing-ly rich! Zack: I'll eat sal-mon.
Eb7 Ab Eb7
Down on Long Is-land, And as a res-i-dent I will pan the Pres-i-dent.
Byng: I'll play back-gam-mon. Girl: Turn break-fast in-to lunch. Whiffen: I'll take Er-rol Flynn to lunch.

Db/Ab Ab Dm7-5 G7 Cm9 Cm(+7) Cm Fm7-5 Bb7
I'll as - pi - re___ High - er___ and high - er.___
Zack: I'll as - pi - re___ High - er___ and high - er.___
f
Eb Bb7 Eb Fm7 Eb/G Ab
I'll get mar - ried and a - dopt a son___ Right from To - ny's or from
Byng: I'll buy au - tos like the au - to - crats.___ Zack: I'll drink Plu - to like the
mf
Gm/Bb Ab/C Bb7 Eb C7 Fm7
Guitar Tacet
Twen - ty - One.__ Swim - ming in high - balls, stewed to the eye - balls, Just dis - gust - ing - ly
plu - to - crats.__ Sandy: Play - ing the hors - es, get - ting di - vorc - es. All: Just dis - gust - ing - ly
f
Fm7 Bb9 1 Eb Bb 2 Eb
rich, Too too dis - gust - ing - ly rich!
rich, Too too dis - gust - ing - ly rich!
sfz

It's A Lovely Day For A Murder

Words by LORENZ HART
Music by RICHARD RODGERS

Moderately Bright
mf
Dm
Bb/D
Have you ev - er heard of Saint Bar - thol - o - mew's Day?
Or the day when we have our tax - es to pay?
Dm
Or the day when they took our li - quor a - way?
Or the day when the Tro - jans were fooled by U -
1
Bb/D

2
Dm
Gm/B♭
lys - ses?
Well, to - day is a
A7
G/B
day that makes those days look like sis - sies.
Cm6
A7/C♯
Dm
Dm7
What a love - ly day for a mur - der,
Dm
Em7-5
A7
I could spit!
If there's

Em7-5
A7
A7+5
Em7-5
A7-9
an - y day for a mur - der,
Em7-5
A7
Dm
this is it! Oh, we'll
D
Dmaj7
D6
Dmaj7
D
nev - er vis - it the par - son,
Dmaj7
Em7
A7
Em7
A7
so I say, For se - duc - tion, rob - b'ry and

Em7
A9
Em7
A7
Dmaj7
ar - son, What a day!
D6
F
F6
Gm7
I could choke my
C7
F
Fmaj7
C9
Am/C
grand - moth - er with her shawl,
E/C
C7
F
F6
Gm7
C7
I could turn Re - pub - li - can in

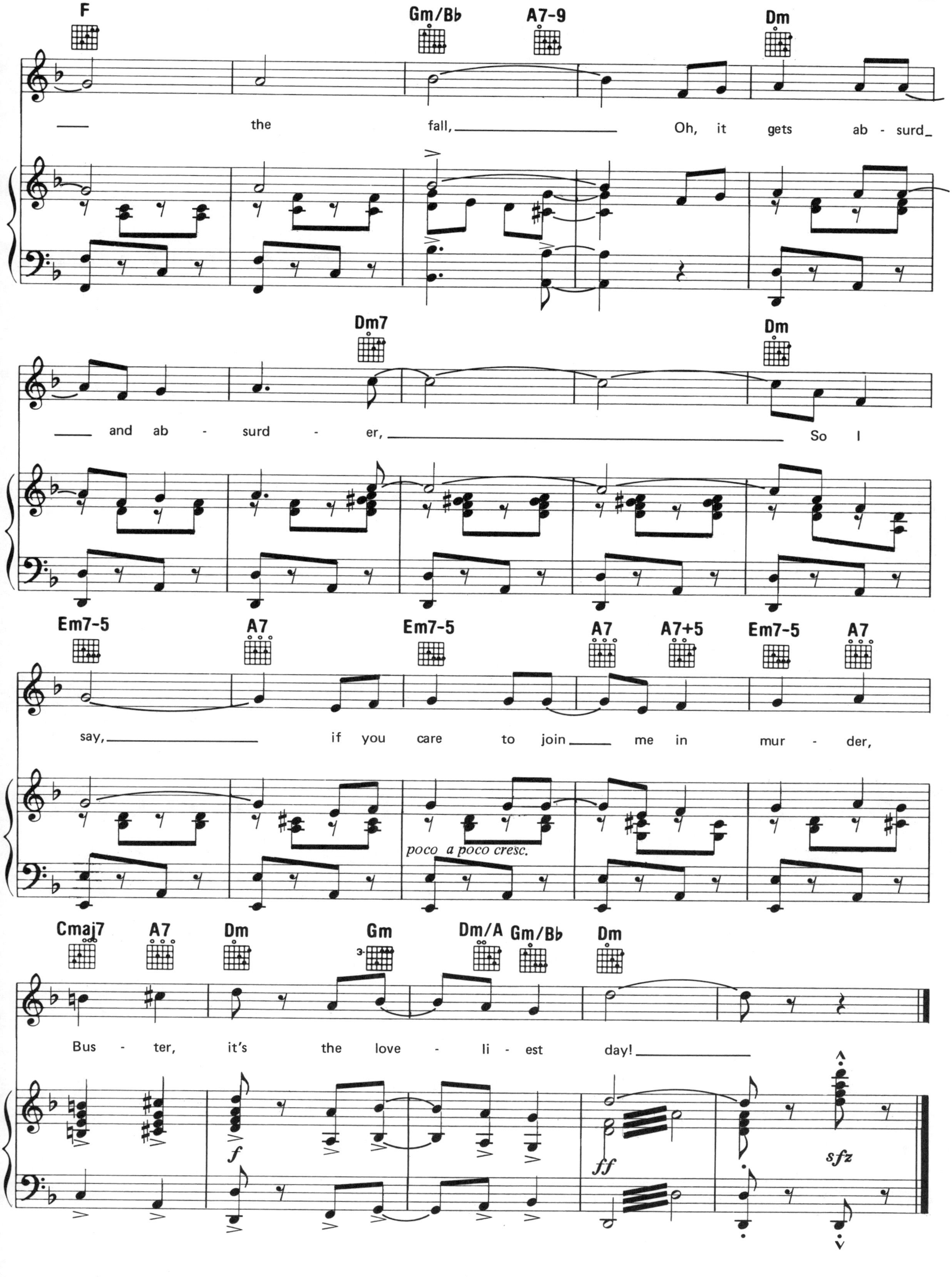
F Gm/B♭ A7-9 Dm
the fall, Oh, it gets ab - surd
Dm7 Dm
and ab - surd - er, So I
Em7-5 A7 Em7-5 A7 A7+5 Em7-5 A7
say, if you care to join me in mur - der,
poco a poco cresc.
Cmaj7 A7 Dm Gm Dm/A Gm/B♭ Dm
Bus - ter, it's the love - li - est day!
f
ff
sfz

It Never Entered My Mind

Words by LORENZ HART
Music by RICHARD RODGERS

With tranquillity
mf
p legato tranquillo
B♭ F B♭6 F B♭ F
I don't care if there's pow-der on my nose, I don't care if my
B♭6 F B♭ F G7
hair-do is in place. I've lost the ver-y mean-ing of re-pose, I
Gm7 C Cm Gm
nev-er put a mud pack on my face. Oh, who'd have thought that I'd

A7
D7
G7
walk in a daze now, I never go to shows at night, But just to mat-in-ees now.
Gm7
C
Cm6
C9
I see the show and home I go.
poco rit.
Refrain (slowly, with warm expression)
F
Am
Once I laughed when I heard you say-ing That I'd be play-ing
p a tempo
sol-i-taire, Un-eas-y in my eas-y chair.

Gm7 Eb7 C7 F Am
It nev - er en-tered my mind. Once you told me
mf
p
F Am F Am F Am
I was mis-tak - en That I'd a-wak - en with the sun
F Am F Am Gm7
And or - der or - ange juice for one, It nev - er en-tered my mind.
C7 F Gm7 C7 Fmaj7 F6 Gm7
You have what I lack my - self,
mf
mp

C7 F C7 F Bdim C7 Gm7 Am
And now I e-ven have to scratch my back my-self,
mf marcato
Bb Am C7 F Am F Am F Am
Once you warned me That if you scorned me, I'd sing the maid-en's
mp
F Am F Am Cm6 Bb+ D7 Gm C7
pray'r a-gain And wish that you were there a-gain To get in-to my
mf
F Bb6 C7 1. F6 G7 C7 2. F6
hair a-gain, It nev-er entered my mind.
mf
p
Ped.

Ev'rybody Loves You

Words by LORENZ HART
Music by RICHARD RODGERS

Moderately
mf
Eb
Eb6
Ab6
Bb7
I won - der what you're dream - ing while you're sleep - ing? I'll nev - er
p
Eb
Bb7
Eb
Eb6
know, you'll nev - er know. Now at last the world can - not come
F7
Ab6
Bb7
Eb
peep - ing In - to the thoughts you call your own.

Ab6 Bb7 Eb Ab6 Bb7
You close your eyes and you're a - lone; You're in a world that's bright and
Eb Eb6 Bb Db7+5 Fm F+ Bb7
new And there is no one in it, but you.
Eb G7 Cm Eb7 Ab Eb
Com - fy and co - zy All the world is
p-mf
Ab6 Bb7 Ab Eb F9 F7
ros - y Ev' - ry - bod - y loves you when you're a -
mp
mf

Bb F7 C#dim Bb7 Eb G7
sleep. Too late to
cresc. f p
Cm Eb7 Ab Eb Ab6 Bb7
start now Tak - ing things a - part now,
mp
Ab Eb F9 F7 Bb F7
Ev'ry - bod - y loves you when you're a - sleep
mf cresc.
C#dim Bb7 Eb7 Ab Db7 Gb
You for - get your Al - pha - bet When
f mp

B7 E Ab Ab6 Bb7
you've been count - ing sheep, Does my dream - er
Eb F7 Bb F7 C#dim Bb7 Eb G7
know trou - bles will keep. Com-fy and
mf cresc.
p
Cm Eb7 Ab Eb Cm F9 Eb Gb
co - zy All the world is ros - y, Ev' - ry - bod - y
cresc.
Cb Abm Eb Fm Bb7 1 Eb B7 2 Eb
loves you when you sleep! sleep!
mf
sf

Have You Met Miss Jones?

Words by LORENZ HART
Music by RICHARD RODGERS

Moderately
mf
p
F Bdim
It hap - pened, I felt it
C7 Bdim Am7 Bdim Gm7 C7
hap - pen. I was a - wake, I was - n't blind. I did - n't
F Bdim C7 Bdim F Bdim Gm7 C7
think, I felt it hap - pen. Now I be - lieve in mat - ter o - ver

F F7 B♭ Edim F F9
mind. And now, you see, we must-n't wait. The near-est
mp
B♭ G7 C7(F) C7
mo-ment that we mar-ry is too late!
rit.
Refrain (gracefully and not fast)
F F♯dim Gm C7 Gm C7
"Have you met Miss Jones?" Some one said as
p a tempo
Gm7 C7 F Dm G7
we shook hands. She was just Miss Jones to

Gm C7 Gm7 C7 C+ F F♯dim
me. Then I said, "Miss Jones,
Gm C7 Gmi C7 Gm7 C7 F Dm G7
You're a girl who un - der-stands I'm a man who must be
Gm7 C7 F7 B♭ D♭7
free." And all at once I lost my breath, And all at
mf
G♭ A7 D
once was scared to death, And all at once I owned the

D♭7(G♭) D♭7 G♭ C7 F
earth and sky! Now I've met Miss
mp
F♯dim Gm C7 Gm C7 Gm7 C7 Fmaj7 Bdim
Jones, And we'll keep on meet- ing till we die,
mf
Gm7 C7 1. F B♭7 F C7(F) C7
Miss Jones and I.
2. F B♭7 F
I.
rall. p

I'd Rather Be Right

Words by LORENZ HART
Music by RICHARD RODGERS

Moderately
mf
rit. e dim.
D
Bb+ D Bb+ D G D
He: When I first got my job they paid me sev - en - teen a
p
a tempo
D7 G C6 A7 Dmaj7 Bm/A
week; In just five years I'm get - ting twen - ty - two.
Em7 A7 D Bb+ D Bb+ D G D
I'll get an - oth - er two buck raise When I've the nerve to

D7 G C6 A7 B7sus B7
speak. She: And if you don't I'll still love you.
F#m7 B7 E7 A11 A13
You're al - ways right no mat - ter what you do.
mf
Guitar Tacet
D Dmaj7 Bm D Em7 A7
I'd rath - er be right than in - flu - en - tial,
p-mf
Em7 A7 Em7 A7 Em7 A7
I'd rath - er be right than wealth - y and

Dmaj7 D7 Bm D Em7 A7 Em7 A7
wise, I don't come through, dear, where brains be -
Dm D Em7 A7
long. But per - tain - ing to you, dear,
mf
Em7 B7+5 E7 A7
Guitar Tacet
I can't go wrong. I'd rath - er be
p
D Dmaj7 Bm7 D Em7 A7
right than pres - i - den - tial,

Em7 A7 Em7 A7 Em7 A7 D11
Let oth - er folks fight for heights a - bove,
D7 G6 D7 G Em
What do I fight for? Just to be right for
Em7-5 D Bm Em7 A7
I'd rath - er be right, Just right a - bout
1 D E9 A7
love! I'd rath - er be
Guitar Tacet
2 D
love!
mf
cresc.
sf

At The Roxy Music Hall

Words by LORENZ HART
Music by RICHARD RODGERS

Moderately
mf
Gm7 C7 F Dm7 G7
Come with me And you won't be - lieve a thing you
Step this way Hear the su - per su - per or - gan
mp
C7 F Gm7 Am Gm
see, Where an ush - er puts his heart in what he ush - es, There the
play, Where they change the lights a mil - lion times a min - ute, Where the
F Gm7 Am Bb7
foun - tain chang - es col - or when it gush - es, Where the
stage goes up and down when they be - gin it It's a

A Bm C♯m D
seats ca - ress your car - cass with their plush - es, At The
won - der Mis - sus Roose - velt is - n't in it! At The
Am F♯dim Gm7 C7 Gm7 C7
Rox - y Mu - sic Hall Hold my
Rox - y Mu - sic Hall Come a -
F Dm7 G7 C7
hand, Don't be fright - ened when you hear that band, They come
long, Hear them sing the Vol - ga Boat - man Song, Where the
F Gm7 Am Gm F Gm7
up like A - li Ba - ba from the cel - lar Through the cour - te - sy of Mis - ter Rock - e -
ac - ro - bats are whirl - ing on their dig - its Where the bal - co - ny's so high you get the

Am Bb7 A Bm C#m D
fel - ler Then they play the o - ver - ture from Wil - liam Tel - ler At The
fidg - ets Where the ac - tors seem to be a lot of mid - gets At The
Am A Gm7 C7 F Bb F7
Rox - y Mu - sic Hall You don't have to read the ad It's
Rox - y Mu - sic Hall If you're lost while climb - ing up And
mf
Bb Cm7 F7 Db
al - ways worth the dough, An - y week you
find the go - ing hard, They are on their
Ab7 Bb Am E C7 F7 Gm7 C7
go It's the same old show. Don't be
guard They send a Saint Ber - nard. Come with
mp

F Dm7 G7 C7
shy, - If a na - ked stat - ue meets your eye, Where the
me Where the drink - ing cups are al - ways free, It's a
F Gm7 Am F7 Bb Cm7
bal - let is so sweet with birds and ros - es, That you break out in a rash be - fore it
won - der - land where ev' - ry - one is A - lice, Where the la - dies room is big - ger than a
Bb Bbm F C+ C7
clos - es, At The Rox - y Mu - sic
pal - ace, At The Rox - y Mu - sic
mf
1 F C7 F6 C7
Hall.
Hall.
2 F C7 F
Hall.
Hall.
sf

Spring Is Here

Words by LORENZ HART
Music by RICHARD RODGERS

Quietly
mf
poco rit.
A♭ Cm D♭ D♭6 E♭7
Once there was a thing called spring, when the world was writ-ing vers-es like
p a tempo
A♭maj7 Cm D♭ A♭ Cm D♭
yours and mine All the lads and girls would sing, When we
D♭6 E♭7 A♭ B♭m A♭ A♭dim
sat at lit - tle ta - bles and drank May wine.

Bbm7 Eb7 Ab Dbmaj7
Now A-pril, May and June are sad-ly out of tune
Bbm7 Eb7
Life has stuck the pin in the bal-loon.
poco rit.
Refrain (slowly, with expression)
Abdim Ab Abdim
Spring is here! Why does-n't my heart go
p-mf a tempo
Ab6 Ab7(b9) Eb9 Ab7(b9)
danc-ing? Spring is here! Why is-n't the waltz en-

E♭9
A♭
D♭
tranc-ing? No de-sire, No am-bi-tion leads
3
A♭
Fm
me, May-be it's be - cause no-bod-y
3
B♭7
E♭7
A♭dim
A♭
needs me. Spring is here!
3
p
A♭dim
A♭6
A♭7 (♭9)
Why does-n't the breeze de - light me? Stars ap -
3

Eb9 Ab7(b9) Eb9
pear Why does-n't the night in - vite me?
Ab Bb7
May - be it's be - cause no - bod - y loves
mf
Eb7(Ab) Eb7 Cm Fm Bbm7 Eb7 1.Ab
me, Spring is here I hear!
Eb7+(b9) Eb7 2.Ab Ab7 Db Ab(Db) Ab
hear!

I Married An Angel

Words by LORENZ HART
Music by RICHARD RODGERS

Moderately
mf
calmly
p semplice
C7 F G7 Gm7 C7 Gm
There's been a change in me! I have a love-ly dis-po-
C7 F G7 Gm7 C7 Gm C7 F
si-tion, That's ver-y strange in me. And life's as sweet as it can be.
Gm7 C7 Gmaj7 F6 Gm7 C7 Fmaj7 F6
I've lots of cour-age and am-bi-tion. From ev-'ry care my mind is free,

Gm6 A7 Dm B♭m6 F C7 F G7(♭5)
So I re-peat, with your per - mis- sion, There's been a change in me!
Refrain (with emphatic feeling)
F C7 F Dm Gm7 C7 F Dm Gm7 C7
Have you heard I mar-ried an an-gel, I'm sure that the
F D7 Gm7 C7 F F C7 F Dm
change 'll be aw-f'lly good for me. Have you heard
Gm7 C7 F Dm Gm7 C7 F D7
An an-gel I mar-ried, To heav-en she's car-ried this
p
mf
p

Gm7 C7 F Dm7 G7 C Dm7 G7
fel-low with a kiss. She is sweet and gen-tle, So it is-n't
sf mf
C Cm7 F7 B♭ F G9 C7 C7(♭9)
strange, When I'm sen-ti - men-tal, She loves me like an an - gel.
F C7 F Dm Gm7 C7 F Dm
Now you've heard, I mar-ried an an-gel,
p
Gm7 C7 F D7 Gm7 C7 1. F C7 2. F
This beau-ti-ful change 'll be aw-f'lly good for me. me.
mf

The Most Beautiful Girl In The World

Music by RICHARD RODGERS
Words by LORENZ HART

Moderate Waltz tempo
mf
Dm7 G7 G+ C Dm7 G7 G+
We used to spend the spring to-geth-er be-fore we learned to
p
C G7 Dm7 G7
walk; We used to
mf
p
G+ C Dm7 G7 C
laugh and sing to-geth-er be-fore we learned how to talk.

G7
C
E
F
G7
B
C
With no rea - son for the sea - son
mf
p
Am7
D7
Dm7
G7
Spring would end as it would start.
mf
C
E
F
G7
B
C
Am7
D7
G
Now the sea - son has a rea - son, And there's spring-time in my heart.
p
cresc.
Guitar tacet
f

Refrain
C7 F Fdim F
The most beau-ti-ful girl in the world Picks my ties out,
p
Fdim F Fdim C7 sus4 C7
eats my can - dy, Drinks my bran - dy, The most beau-ti-ful
F Am Gm7 C7 F
girl in the world. The most beau-ti-ful star in the
mf
Fdim F Fdim F Fdim C7 sus4 C7
world is - n't Gar - bo, Is - n't Diet - rich But the sweet trick

Cm Cm6 D7
who can make me be-lieve it's a beau-ti-ful world.
cresc.
mf
Dm G9 Cm7 C7 Dm G9
So - cial not a bit, Nat - 'ral kind of
Gm7 C7 Am7 D7 G7 sus 4 G7
wit, She'd shine an - y - where And she
Gm7 C Gm C7 F
has-n't got plat-i-num hair The most beau-ti-ful house in the
p

Fdim F Fdim F Fdim
world Has a mort - gage what do I care, it's good-
C7 sus 4 C7 Cm
bye care When my slip-pers are next to the ones that be - long
cresc.
Cm6 D7 Dm7 G7 Gm7 Bb7
To the one and on - ly beau-ti-ful girl in the
f
1. F Bb F C7 2. F Bb F
world! The most world!
mf
f

Little Girl Blue

Words by LORENZ HART
Music by RICHARD RODGERS

Moderately
F Dm7 Bbmaj7 C9 F F7-9 Bb
Sit there and count your fin - gers, what can you do? Old girl you're
Sit there and count the rain - drops fall - ing on you. It's time you
Bbm F Eb7 D7 Db7 Am7 Ab7 Gm7 C9
through. Sit there and count your lit - tle fin - gers, Un - luck - y Lit - tle Girl
knew, all you can count on is the rain - drops That fall on Lit - tle Girl
1 F Ab G Gb
Blue.
2 F Ab G Gb F C7
Blue. No use, old girl, you
F Asus A7
may as well sur - ren - der. Your hope is get - ting slen - der, Why won't some - bod - y

Dm7 D7-9 Gm7 C7 F Bbmaj7 C9 F Ab
send a ten - der Blue boy to cheer a lit - tle girl blue?
G Gb F Gm7 C7 F
When I was ver - y young the world was young - er than
strung with ev - 'ry star in the
Am7 Ab7 Gm7 C7 F
I, As mer - ry as a car - ou - sel The cir - cus tent was
sky A - bove the ring I loved so well.
Dm7 Gm7 F
Now the young world has grown old, Gone are the
C7
tin - sel and gold.
D.S. al Coda
CODA
F Ab G Gb F
Blue?

My Romance

Words by LORENZ HART
Music by RICHARD RODGERS

Moderately
mf
poco rit.
Em6 D7 Em6 D7 Em6 D7 Em6 D7
I won't kiss your hand, Ma - dam, Cra - zy for you though I am.
p a tempo
G7 C7 F Fm C G7 C
I'll nev-er woo you on bend-ed knee, No Ma-dam, not me.
Em6 D7 Em6 D7 G Dm7 G7
We don't need that flow-'ry fuss, No sir, Ma-dam, not for us.

Refrain (smoothly with expression)
C C F C
My ro - mance does-n't have to have a moon in the sky, My ro-
p-mf
Am Cmaj7 F C Dm7 G7 C F
mance does-n't need a blue la - goon stand-ing by; No month of
mf
C C9 F C F♯m7 B7 Em Am
May, no twin - kling stars, no hide a - way, no
G D7 G sus4 G7 C
soft gui - tars. My ro - mance does-n't need a cas - tle
p

F C Am Cmaj7 F C
ris - - ing in Spain, Nor a dance to a con-stant-ly sur-
Dm7 G7 C C7 F A7 Dm
pris - - ing re-frain. Wide a-wake I can make my most fan-
cresc.
E7 A7 D7 C Am Dm7 G7
tas-tic dreams come true; My ro-mance does-n't need a thing but
mf
f
dim.
1. C D7 G7 2. C
you. My ro- you.
mf
Ped.

Love Me Tonight

Words by LORENZ HART
Music by RICHARD RODGERS

Moderately
mf
F
Vamp
mp
There's a glis - ten-ing
Gm7 F Gm F
ring a - round the moon.
Are you lis - ten - ing,
Gm7 F Gm F D7
it is not too soon!
G7-5 G7 C7-9 C7 F7+5
Must we sleep to-night all a -

Bbmaj9 Gm7-5 F G7 C7sus C7 F
lone? Let us keep to-night as our ver - y own.
Dm Am C7
Your heart and my heart were made to meet,
p-mf
F Bdim Gm7 C7 F
Don't make them wait; Love me to - night! Why should our
3
Dm Am G#dim A E7sus E7
lips be a - fraid to meet? Love me to -
3

A A7 Bb+ D7 Cm7 D7 Gm
night! Who knows what to - mor - row brings
Cm Bb Am C7 F C7sus C7
With the morn - ing light.
F Dm Am G#dim D7 Gm Gm7
Dear, I am here with a heart that sings, Love me
C7 F Db7 C7 F
to - night. night.

Isn't It Romantic?

Words by LORENZ HART
Music by RICHARD RODGERS

Calmly
mp
p
Ab
Abm
I've never met you, Yet never
My face is glowing, I'm ener-
Eb
Adim
Fm7
Bb7+5
Ebmaj7
doubt, dear, I can't forget you, I've thought you out dear, I know your
getic, The art of sewing, I found poetic, My needle
Ab
Bb7
Eb
C7
profile and I know the way you kiss just the thing I
punctuates the rhythm of romance! I don't give a

Fm Bb7 Eb Ab Abm
miss on a night like this. If dreams are made of im-ag-i-
stitch, if I don't get rich. A cus-tom tai-lor who has no
Eb Adim Fm7 Bb+ Ebmaj7
na-tion, I'm not a-fraid of my own cre-a-tion. With all my
cus-tom, Is like a sail-or, no one will trust 'em. But there is
Ab Bb7 Eb Adim Bb7 Eb6 F7 Bb7
heart, my heart is here for you to take. Why should I quake? I'm not a-wake.
mag-ic in the mu-sic of my shears; I shed no tears. Lend me your ears!
Refrain (with simplicity)
Bb7 Eb Bb7 Ab Bb7 Eb Bb+7
Is-n't it ro-man-tic? Mu-sic in the night, A dream that can be
Is-n't it ro-man-tic? Soon I will have found some girl that I a-
p

Eb Bb7 Eb Bb7 Ab Bb7 Eb
heard. Is-n't it ro-man-tic? Mov-ing shad-ows write the old-est mag-ic
dore. Is-n't it ro-man-tic? While I sit a-round, my love can scrub the
C7+ C7 Fm C7 Fm Bb7 G7 Cm G7+
word. I hear the breez-es play-ing in the trees a-
floor. She'll kiss me ev-'ry hour, — or she'll get the
Cm Eb7 Ab C7 Fm Bb7 Bdim Cm F9
bove. While all the world is say-ing you were meant for
sack. And when I take a show-er she can scrub my
Edim Bb7 Eb Bb7 Ab Bb7
love. Is-n't it ro-man-tic? Mere-ly to be young on
back. Is-n't it ro-man-tic? On a moon-light night she'll

E♭ B♭+7 E♭ B♭7 E♭ B♭7 A♭ B♭7
such a night as this? Is-n't it ro-man-tic? Ev-'ry note that's sung is
cook me on-ion soup. Kid-dies are ro-man-tic, And if we don't fight, we
E♭ C7+5 C7 Fm C7 Fm B♭7 G7
like a lov-er's kiss. Sweet sym-bols in the moon-light,
soon will have a troupe! We'll help the pop-u-la-tion,
Cm Cm7 Cm6 A♭m6 E♭ C♯dim B♭7
Do you mean that I will fall in love per-chance? Is-n't it ro-
It's a du-ty that we owe to dear old France. Is-n't it ro-
f
1. E♭ Adim B♭7
mance? Is-n't it ro-
2. E♭ A♭m6 E♭
mance?
mf

Lover

Words by LORENZ HART
Music by RICHARD RODGERS

Moderate waltz tempo
mf
C
Dm7
G7
C
When you held your hand to my heart, Dear, you did
p
G7
C
some - - thing grand to my heart, And we played the
A7
D7
G7
Am
scene to per - fec - tion, Though we did - n't have

D7 Em G7 C
time to re - hearse. Since you took con -
Dm7 G7 C
trol of my life You have be - come the
B7 Em Am D7 Gmaj7
whole of my life. When you are a - way it's aw -
Em Am D7 G B G7
ful And when you are with me it's worse.
p

Refrain (very vivaciously and spiritedly)
C B♭7 sus e B7 B♭7 sus e♭
Lov - er, when I'm near you And I hear you
Lov - er, when I'm near you And I hear you
mf
B♭7 A7 sus d A7 A♭7 sus d♭ A♭7
speak my name Soft - ly in my
speak my name Soft - ly in my
G7 sus c G7 C F G7
ear you breathe a flame.
ear you breathe a flame.
C B7 sus e B7 B♭7 sus e♭ B♭7
Lov - er, when we're danc - ing keep on glanc - ing in my
Lov - er, it's im - mor - al, but why quar - rel with our
mf

A7sus d A7 A♭7sus d♭ A♭7 G7sus c G7
eyes, Till Love's own en - tranc - ing mu - sic
bliss, When two lips of cor - al want to
C E
dies. All of my fu - ture is
kiss? I say "The Dev - il is
mf
B7sus e B7 E B7sus e B7
in you. Your ev - 'ry plan I de - sign
in you." And to re - sist you I try;
G D7sus g D7 Em F♯dim
Prom - ise you'll al - ways con - tin - ue to be mine.
But if you did - n't con - tin - ue I would die!
f

Dm7 G7 C B7 sus e B7
Lov - er, please be ten - der, When your
Lov - er, please be ten - der, When your
mf
Bb7 sus eb Bb7 A7 sus d A7 Ab7 sus db
ten - der fears de - part, Lov - er,
ten - der fears de - part, Lov - er,
Ab7 G7 sus c G7 Dm ten. G7 ten. 1. C Dm7
I sur - ren - der to my heart.
I sur - ren - der to my heart.
ten. ten.
a tempo
cresc.
G7 2. C Dm C
heart.
heart.
f
cresc.
sf
Led.

Mimi

Words by LORENZ HART
Music by RICHARD RODGERS

Very gaily, but in moderate tempo
mf
G D7 G D7 Am7 D7
My left shoe's on my right foot, My right shoe's on my left. Oh!
p
G Ddim D7
lis - ten to me Mi - mi, Of rea - son I'm be - reft! The
G D7 G A7 D7 G
but-tons of my trou-sers Are but-ton'd to my vest; Oh! lis - ten to me

Em7 A7 Em7 A7 Am7 D7
Mi-mi, Mere pas - sion's in my breast!
Refrain
G(A) G Am7 D7 Gmaj7
Mi-mi, You fun-ny lit-tle good for noth-ing Mi-mi,
p
G6 Am7 D7 G(A) G
Am I the guy? Mi-mi, You
Am7 D7 Gmaj7 G6 Dm7
sun-ny lit-tle hon-ey of a Mi-mi, I'm aim-ing high!

G7 C(B) C Cdim
Mi-mi, You've got me sad and dream - y,
mf
G6 Gdim G(A)
You could free — me, If you'd see — me, Mi-mi,
G Am7 D7 G C6 G C6
You know I'd like to have a lit-tle son of a Mi-mi bye and
1. G Am7 D7
bye. —
2. G Am7 G
bye. —
mf
f

Any Old Place With You

Music by RICHARD C. RODGERS
Lyric by LORENZ M. HART

Brightly
mf
mp
F
C7
F
C7
There is a rail-road a-round lov-er's lane
We'll mad-ly fly o-ver hill and down dale
F
C7
F
C7
And the con-duc-tor is you.
In lit-tle Cu-pid's ex-press.
F
C7
F
My heart goes fast-er than an-y old train,
I'm at the throt-tle and I'll nev-er fail,

Dm7 G7 C C7
Right on sched - - ule too.
If you whis - - per "yes."
Am7 D7 Am7 D7 G
All is read - y for our hon - ey - moon,
Come with me and let me be your guide,
Am7 D7 Am7 D7 G D+ G
I've a route in view.
One plus one is one.
Am7 D7 Am7 D7 G
Our ex - press leaves morn - ing night and noon,
Then our head - lights nev - er can col - lide,

Am D7 G Gdim G7 G+
Trav - el with me please do.
Till life's long road is done.
Refrain (in strict 4/4)
C
We'll melt in Syr - i - a, freeze in Si - be - ri - a,
From old Vir - gin - i - a, or Ab - ys - sin - i - a,
mf
F Ab7 C G7 Dm
Neg - li - gee in Tim - buk - tu, In dream - y Por - tu - gal
We'll go straight to Hal - i - fax, I've got a ma - ni - a
G7 Gdim G7 Cdim C Cdim G7
I'm goin' to court you gal, an - cient Rome we'll paint a - new.
for Penn - syl - va - ni - a, e - ven ride in Lon - don hacks.

C
Life would be cheer - i - er on Lake Su - pe - ri - or,
I'll call each dude a pest, you like in Bu - da - pest,
mf
F Ab7 C A7 Dm Cdim
How would Pe - kin do? I'm goin' to cor - ner ya
Oh for far Pe - ru! I'll go to hell for ya
f
3
mf
C Am G7
in Cal - i - for - ni - a, An - y old place with
or Phil - a - del - phi - a, An - y old place with
1. C Cdim G7
you.
2. C Fm C
you.
f
3

It's Easy To Remember

Words by LORENZ HART
Music by RICHARD RODGERS

Slowly
p
Fm7 Bb7 Eb Fm7 Bb7 Eb6 Eb7
With you I owned the earth. With you I ruled cre - a - tion. No
mp
Ab Fm7-5 Eb Abm F7 F7-5 Bb7
you, and what's it worth? It's just an im - i - ta - tion.
rall.
p
Slowly and expressively
Guitar Tacet
Fm7 Bb7 Eb Fm7 Bb7
Your sweet ex - pres - sion, the smile you gave me, the way you looked when we
mp

Eb Eb+ Abm Ab Eb Fm7 Adim Eb Bb9
met. It's eas - y to re - mem - ber but so hard to for -
Eb Fm7 Bb7 Eb Fm7 Bb7
get. I hear you whis - per, "I'll al - ways love you." I know it's o - ver and
Eb Eb+ Abm Ab Eb Fm7 Adim Eb Bb9
yet, it's eas - y to re - mem - ber but so hard to for -
Eb Eb7sus Eb7 Abmaj7 Ab6 Bbm7 Eb7
get. So I must dream to have your hand ca - ress me, fin - gers press me

Abmaj7 Ab6 Abm7 Db7 Gbmaj7 Gb6 Bb Cm F7
tight. I'd rath-er dream than have that lone-ly feel-ing steal-ing through the
Bb Bb7 Fm7 Bb7 Eb
night. Each lit-tle mo-ment is clear be-fore me, and though it
Fm7 Bb7 Eb Eb+ Abm Ab Eb Db9
brings me re-gret, it's eas-y to re-mem-ber and
1 Adim Eb Bb9 Eb
so hard to for-get. Your sweet ex-
2 Adim Eb Bb9 Eb Ab Eb
so hard to for-get.
mp
rall.

Soon

Words by LORENZ HART
Music by RICHARD RODGERS

Moderately

mf
F C7sus C7 F C7 Dm7 G7 C F C7sus C7
Ev'-ry day that I'm with-out you, seems a year. Yet I let each
mp
F C7 Dm7 G7 C7sus C7 F G F G
fear a-bout you dis-ap-pear. Days that part us
F G7 C F C F C F G7
will be few, And I know with-out a doubt you feel it

Am E C7 F C7 F
too. Soon, may-be not to - mor - row but soon, There'll just be
mp -mf
C7sus C7 F C7 F
two of us, Soon you and I will bor - row the moon for just the
D7sus D7 G D7 G
two of us. Sweet - ly and so dis - creet - ly We'll be com-plete - ly a -
D7 F C7 F Bdim C7
lone; No oth - er world, On - ly our own.

F C7 F C7sus C7 Eb F7
Now we must be con - tent - ed with schemes a - bout the two of us.
Bb F7 Bb D7+5(b9) D7-9 D7-5 D7
Yet we can have our sweet scent - ed dreams, That will come true of us, for
Gm Gm7 Bbm Bbm6 F Bb7 F
pres-ent-ly and pleas-ant-ly our hearts will be in tune. So, soon, may be not to -
C7sus C7 1 F G7-5 Am C7 2 F
mor - row, but soon. soon.
mp

Glad To Be Unhappy

Words by LORENZ HART
Music by RICHARD RODGERS

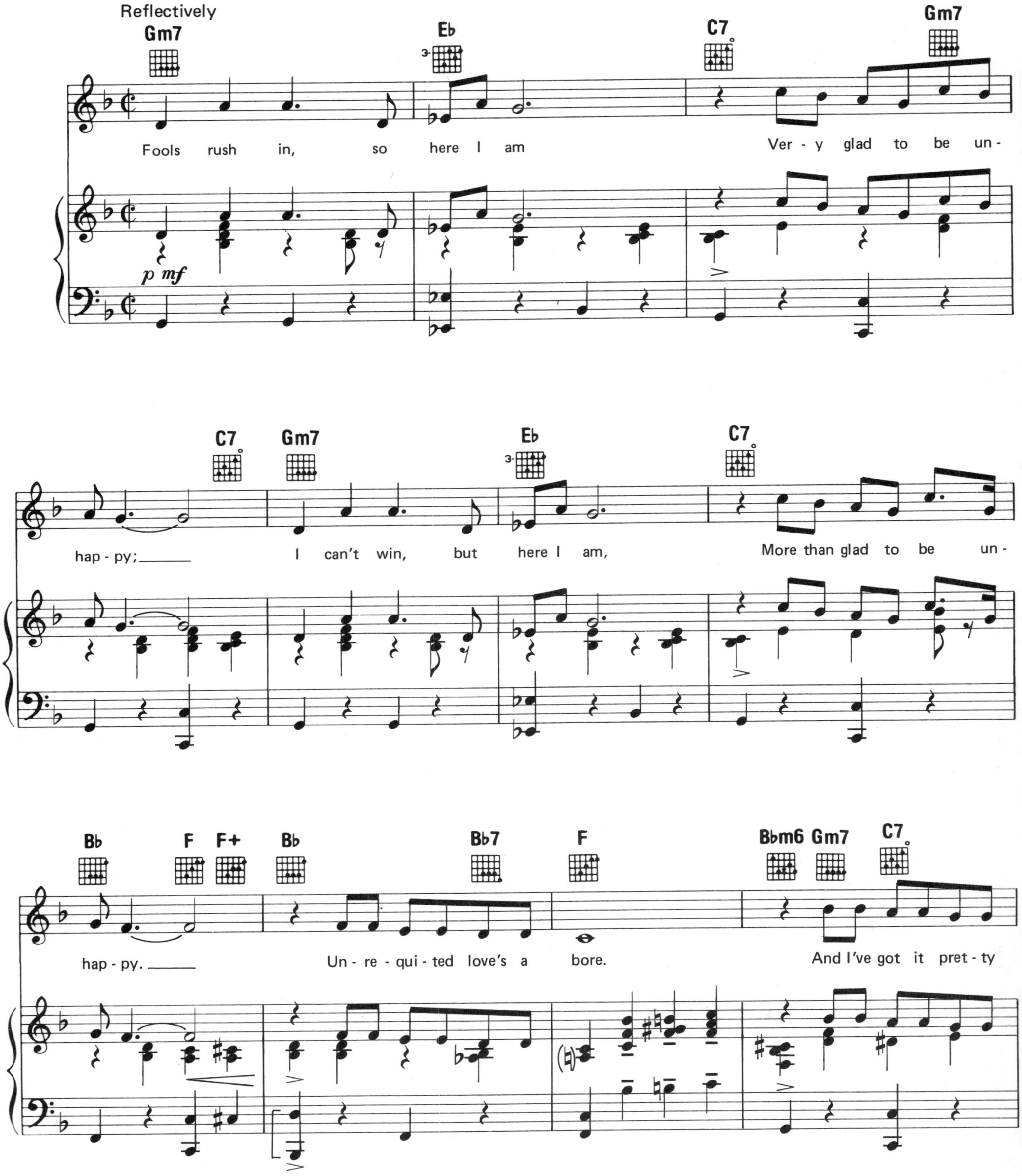
Reflectively
Gm7 Eb C7 Gm7
Fools rush in, so here I am Ver - y glad to be un -
p mf
C7 Gm7 Eb C7
hap - py; I can't win, but here I am, More than glad to be un -
Bb F F+ Bb Bb7 F Bbm6 Gm7 C7
hap - py. Un - re - qui - ted love's a bore. And I've got it pret - ty

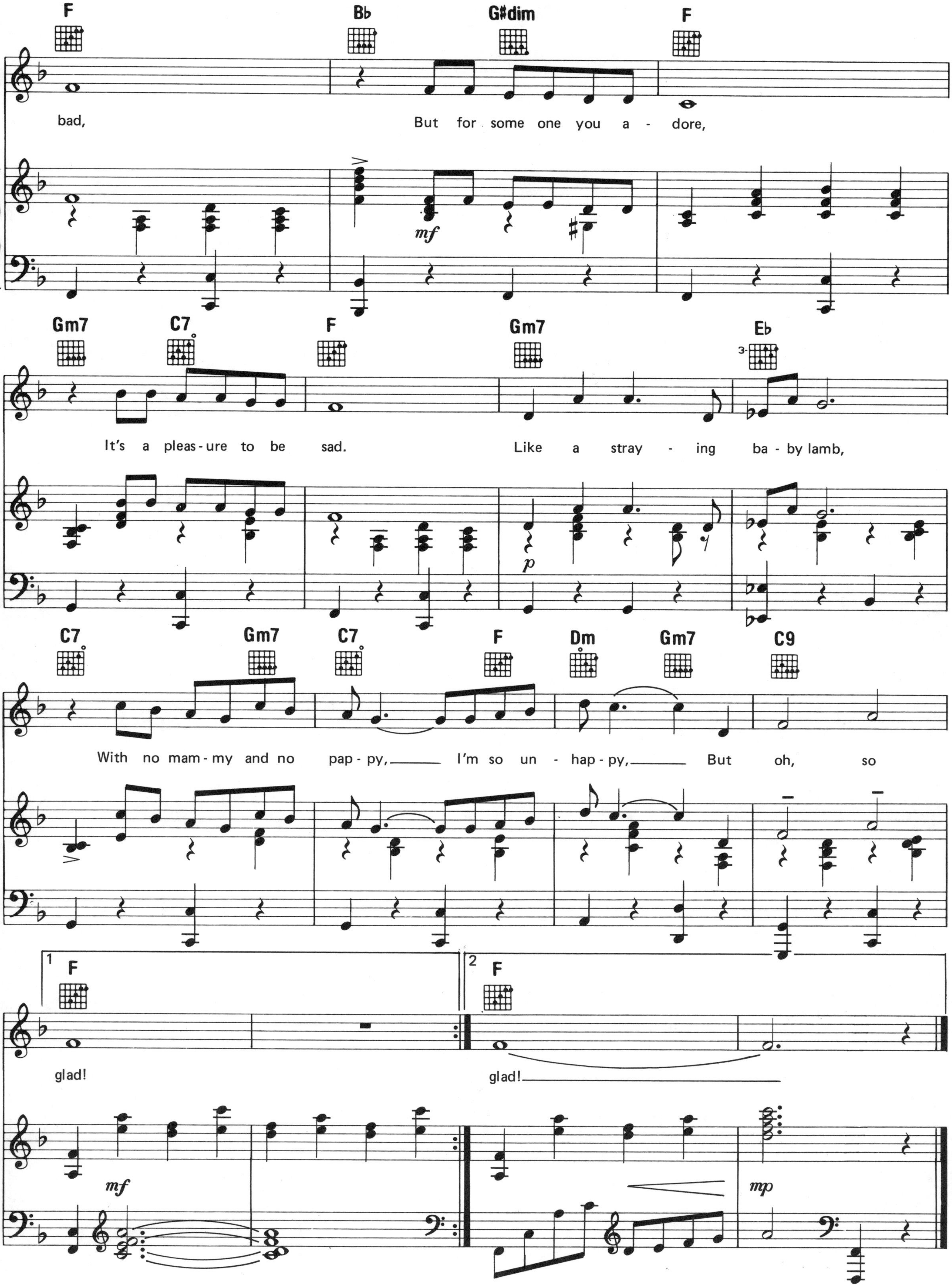
F Bb G#dim F
bad, But for some one you a - dore,
Gm7 C7 F Gm7 Eb
It's a pleas - ure to be sad. Like a stray - ing ba - by lamb,
C7 Gm7 C7 F Dm Gm7 C9
With no mam - my and no pap - py, I'm so un - hap - py, But oh, so
1 F 2 F
glad! glad!
mf p mf mp

Quiet Night

Words by LORENZ HART
Music by RICHARD RODGERS

Smooth 2
F Dm7 G7 Gm7 C7 F7sus F7
Qui - et night, and all a - round the
p – mf
Bbmaj7 Dm7 G7 Gm7 C7 Gm7 C9 F
calm and balm - y weath - er.
Qui - et
Dm7 G7 Gm7 C7 F7sus F7 Bbmaj7 Dm7 G7
night, no oth - er sound but hearts that beat to -

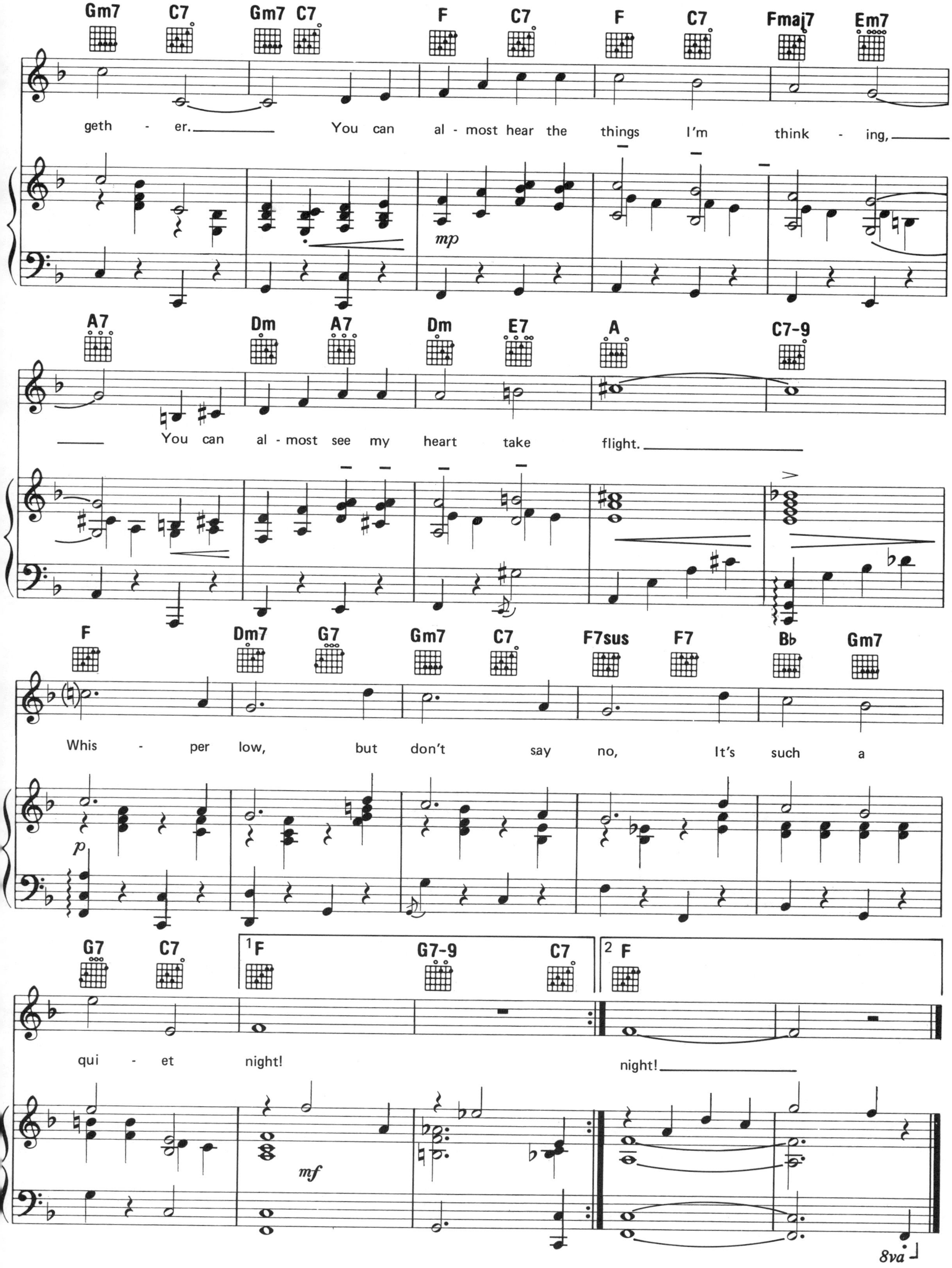

Gm7 C7 Gm7 C7 F C7 F C7 Fmaj7 Em7
geth - er. You can al - most hear the things I'm think - ing,
mp
A7 Dm A7 Dm E7 A C7-9
You can al - most see my heart take flight.
F Dm7 G7 Gm7 C7 F7sus F7 Bb Gm7
Whis - per low, but don't say no, It's such a
p
G7 C7 1 F G7-9 C7 2 F
qui - et night! night!
mf
8va

There's A Small Hotel

Words by LORENZ HART
Music by RICHARD RODGERS

Moderately bright
mp
poco rit.
Am7 F♯ G Am7 F♯
She: I'd like to get a - way, Jun-ior, Some-where a - lone with
p a tempo
G Am7 D7 F♯ Am7 D7
you. It could be oh, so gay, Jun-ior! You need a laugh or
G Am7 F♯ G
two. He: A cer-tain place I know, Frank-ie,

Am7 B♭+ Gmaj7 G6 Am7 D7
Where fun-ny peo-ple can have fun. That's where we two will
B7 B7(♭5) E7 A7 D7 Fdim Am7 rit. D7
go, Darling, Be-fore you can count up One, Two,- Three. For:
rit.
Refrain (leisurely)
Gmaj7 G6 Gmaj7 G6 G
There's a small ho-tel with a wish-ing well; I
mp
Am7 D7 Gmaj7 G6 Gmaj7 G6
wish that we were there to-geth-er.
mf

Gmaj7 G6 Gmaj7 G6 G
There's a brid - al suite; One room bright and neat, com -
p
Am7 D7 Gmaj7 G6 Gmaj7 G6
plete for us to share to - geth - er.
mf
C Dm7 G7 C D♯dim Bm7 E7
Look-ing through the win - dow you can see a dis - tant stee - ple;
mp
Am Bm7 E7 F Am Cm6 D7
Not a sign of peo - ple, Who wants peo - ple?

Gmaj7 G6 Gmaj7 G6 G
When the stee-ple bell says "Good - night, sleep well," we'll
mp
Am7 D7 Gmaj7 G6 Am7 D7
1.
thank the small ho - tel to - geth - er.
mf
2.
Am7 D7 B♭ Cm7 F7
tel. We'll creep in - to our lit - tle shell And we will
poco a poco cresc.
G Am7 D7 Gmaj7
thank the small ho - tel to - geth - er.
rit.
f
L.H.
mf
Ped.

It's Got To Be Love

Words by LORENZ HART
Music by RICHARD RODGERS

Moderately
Bb6 Eb C7 Gm7 C7 Fm7 Bb7
It's got to be love, It could-n't be ton-sil-i-tis,
p – mf
Fm7 Bb7 Eb7 Ab
It feels like neur-i-tis, But
Ab6 G7 Dm7 G7 Bdim Cm Eb7
nev-er-the-less it's love. Don't tell me the pick-les and

Ab
Fm7
Bb7
C7
Gm7
Gm7
C7
pie a la mode, They served me Un -
mp
Fm7
Bb7
Fm7
Bb7
Eb7
Ab
nerved me And made my heart a
Abm6
Bb7
Eb
C7
Gm7
C7
brok - en down pump. It's got to be love, It
Fm7
Bb7
Fm7
Bb7
Eb7
Ab
is - n't the morn - ing af - ter That makes ev' - ry raft - er

Ab6 G7 Dm7 G7 Bdim
Go spin-ning a-round a-bove. I'm
Cm Eb7 Ab Fm7 G7 Cm7 C7+5
sure that it's fat-al, or why do I get That sink - ing
sub. p
mf
F9 Bb7-9 Eb C7 Fm7 Bb7
feel - ing? I think that I'm dead, But nev-er-the-less it's on - ly love.
1 Eb F7-5 Bb7
2 Eb Db9 Ebmaj7
It's
mf
f

Where's That Rainbow?

Words by LORENZ HART
Music by RICHARD RODGERS

Moderately
f
dim. e rall.
very calmly
C G7 C
She: Trou - bles real - ly are bub - bles, they say, And I'm
He: For - tune nev - er smiles, but in my case It just
p a tempo
F C G7 C G7
bub - bling o - ver to - day! Spring brings ros - es to
laughs right in my face. She: If I looked for a
p
C F C G7
peo - ple, you see, But it brings hay fe - ver to me!
horse-shoe, I s'pose It would bop me right in the nose.

C Am D G7
If I have ev - er had luck, It's
My luck will var - y sure - ly, that's
Am D7 Am D7 G G7
bad luck, that's sure. My Po - ly - an - na
pure - ly a curse. My luck has changed, it's
C Cm G6 Am7 D7 G G7
stuff too, Is tough to en - dure!
got - ten From rot - ten to worse!
rit.
Refrain (slowly with tender expression)
C Dm7 G7
Where's that rain - bow you hear a - bout?
p

Where's that lin - ing they cheer a - bout?
Where's that love-nest, where
love is king, ev - er af - ter?
Where's that blue room they sing a - bout?
Where's that sun - shine they fling a - bout?

C Dm G7 C F
I know morning will come, but pardon my laugh - ter!
mf
C F C F Fm Fdim
In each sce-na-ri-o, you can de-pend on the
f mf
C G7 C F
end, where the lov-ers a-gree. Where's that Lo-tha-ri-o,
Fdim C G7 C Dm7 G7
where does he roam with his dome, vas-e-lined as can be?

C Dm7 G7
It is eas - y to see al - right, —
mp
C Dm7 G7 C
Ev - 'ry - thing's gon - na be al - right, — Be just dan - dy for
Dm G7
ev - 'ry - bod - y but me!
1. C F6 C F C G7
fz fz f
me!
2. C F C F C G7 C
me!
f poco a poco dim.

A Tree In The Park

Words by LORENZ HART
Music by RICHARD RODGERS

Leisurely
mf
rit.
p a tempo
F C7
When the nois - y town
We'll make ev - 'ry bough
F C7 F C7 F C7
Lets its win-dows down, Lit - tle slaves are free at night;
Shake, and won-der how Two could be so near - ly one.
D♭ A♭7 D♭ A♭7
Then we'll soon re - treat From the bus - y street,
Ev - 'ry blade of grass Sad - ly sighs, "A - las!"

Db Ab7 Db Gm7 C7
Till the crowds are out of sight. There's a ren-dez-vous for
Grass can nev-er have such fun. In the des-ert town's o-
F Bb F A7 Dm Bbm6 F C7
lov-ers, Where we two can play, Ver-y near your door,
a-sis, We'll love 'neath the tree; It can't be a-miss
F G7 F Dm7 G7 Gm7 C7
In the cit-y's core, But it seems a mil-lion miles a-way.
If the bird-ies kiss; We're as good as birds, aren't we?
rit.
Refrain (liltingly)
F Bb F Gm C7 Gm C7
Meet me un-der-neath our lit-tle tree in the park!
p-mf
a tempo

F Bb F Dm7 G7 Dm7 G7
No one else a - round, but you and me in the dark!
Gm7 C7 Gm Fmaj7 F6 Gm7 C7
Just five min-utes from your door- step, I'll wait for your step to come a -
F F7 Bb F C7 F C7 F
long! And the cit - y's roar be-comes a song!
mf
C7 F Bb F Gm C7
While I'm wait-ing, I dis-cov- er more in your charms;
p

Gm7 C7 F Eb7 Eb
Sud-den-ly I turn a-round, and you're in my arms.
Gm7 C7 Gm Fmaj7 F6
And if there's a moon a-bove you, I'll carve "I
Gm7 C7 F F7 Bb Bbm F Gm C7
love you," up-on the bark, Un-der-neath our lit-tle tree, in-side the
1. F Dm Gm7 C9
park!
2. F Bb6 F
park!
mf
rit.
mf

Bewitched

Words by LORENZ HART
Music by RICHARD RODGERS

Moderately
mf
poco rit.
(not fast)
p a tempo
Dm7 G7 Cmaj7 C6 Dm7 G7 Cmaj7 A7(♭9)
He's a fool and don't I know it, But a fool can have his charms;
Dm7 G7 Cmaj7 C6 Dm7 G7 Cmaj7 C6
I'm in love and don't I show it, Like a babe in arms.
Dm7 G7 Cmaj7 C6 Dm7 G7 C A7(♭9)
Love's the same old sad sen-sa-tion, Late-ly I've not slept a wink,

Dm7 G7 Cmaj7 C6 Dm7 G7
Since this half-pint im-i-ta-tion, Put me on the blink.
rit.
Refrain (slowly, but not dragging)
C G7 C C+
I'm wild a-gain, Be-guiled a-gain, a sim-per-ing, whim-per-ing
p a tempo
F G♯dim C D7 G7 A7
child a-gain, Be-witched, both-ered and be-wil-dered am
Dm G7 C G7
I. Could-n't sleep, and would-n't sleep, When
mf
p

C C+ F G♯dim C D7
love came and told me I should-n't sleep, Be - witched, both-ered and be -
G7 C7 F A7
wil - dered am I.
Dm Dm7 Am
Lost my heart, but what of it? He is cold, I a -
mp
Dm7 G7 G7 Dm7 G7
gree, He can laugh, but I love it, Al - though the

Em7 F♯dim Dm7 G7 C G7
laugh's on me. I'll sing to him, each spring to him, And
mf
p
C C+ F G♯dim C D7
long for the day when I'll cling to him, Be - witched, both-ered and be -
Dm G7 1. C Am Dm7 G7
wil - dered am I. I'm
2. C F C
I.
sf

I Could Write A Book

Words by LORENZ HART
Music by RICHARD RODGERS

Moderately
mf
poco rit.
G Gmaj7 G7 C Cm G A7 D7
A B C D E F G I nev - er learned to spell, at least not
p a tempo
G(c) G Dm G G Gmaj7 G7 C
well. One, two, three, four, five, six sev - en, I
Cm G A7 D7 G(c) G Dm G
nev - er learned to count a great a - mount.

Gm7 C7 Fmaj7 Em7 A7
But my bus - y mind is burn-ing to use what learn-ing I've got,
D7 Gmaj9 G G7 Dm7 G7
I won't waste an - y time, I'll strike while the i - ron is hot.
Refrain (slowly, with expression)
C G7 C Cmaj7
If they asked me I could write a book,
p
C6 G7 C G7 C C♯dim
A - bout the way you walk and whis - per and

Dm7 G7 Dm7 G7 C A♭7 Dm7 G7
look; I could write a pref-ace on
mf più espress.
C F♯dim G C F♯dim G E♭7 Am7 D7
how we met, so the world would nev-er for-
G Dm7 G7 C G7
get, And the sim - ple se-cret of the
mf
p
C Cmaj7 C6 G7 C G7
plot is just to tell them that I

C C♯dim Dm7 G7 Dm7 G7
love you a lot, Then the
più espress.
C A♭7 Dm7 G7 Gm7 C7
world dis - cov - ers as my book
F Dm C C+ Dm7 G7
ends, How to make two lov - ers of
1. C Dm7 G7 2. C F C
friends. If they friends.
mf

You Mustn't Kick It Around

Words by LORENZ HART
Music by RICHARD RODGERS

Moderately
G
Gm7
D7
G
If my heart gets in your hair,
You mus - n't kick it a - round
p-mf
D7
G
Gm7
D7
If you're bored with this af - fair
You mus - n't kick it a - round,
G
D7
G
D7
Ev - en though I'm mild and meek,
When we have a

G
E7
A
A7
Guitar Tacet
brawl. If I turn the oth - er cheek You mus-n't kick it at all.
D7
G
Gm
D7
G
When I try to ring the bell, You nev-er care for the sound,
p
cresc.
Dm7
G7
C
Cm7
D7
The next guy may not do as well, You mus - n't kick
mf
1 G
D7
2 G
Am7
G
it a - round.
round.
f

Happy Hunting Horn

Words by LORENZ HART
Music by RICHARD RODGERS

March Tempo

f
Bb7
mp
Don't wor - ry, girls, I'm on - ly on va - ca - tion, not out of cir - cu - la - tion
Fm7 Bb7
Don't wor - ry, girls. Don't wor - ry, girls, while I still have my eye - sight, you're
Fm7 Eb Fm C7
going to be in my sight. Don't wor - ry, girls. You nev - er can e -

Abmaj7 Fm Abm6 Bb7 Eb
rase the hun - ter from the chase.
Brightly
Eb Bb Eb Bb7 Eb
Sound the hap - py hunt - ing horn, There's new game on the
Bb7 Eb Bb7 Eb Bb7 Eb
trail now, We're hunt - ing for quail now
Bb Eb Bb7 Bbdim Bb7 Eb
Hap - py lit - tle hunt - ing horn. Play the horn but
mf
f

Bb Eb Bb7 Eb Bb7 Eb Bb7 Eb
don't play corn, the mu - sic must be nice now We're hunt - ing for
Bb7 Eb Bb Eb Db B7 Eb7 Ab
mice now Hap - py lit - tle hunt - ing horn. Dan - ger's eas - y
mf
f
Eb Bb Eb Eb6 Eb
to en - dure when you're out to catch a beaut;
f
Ab Eb Ab Eb Ab Eb
Lie in am - bush but be sure, When you see the whites of their
mf
3

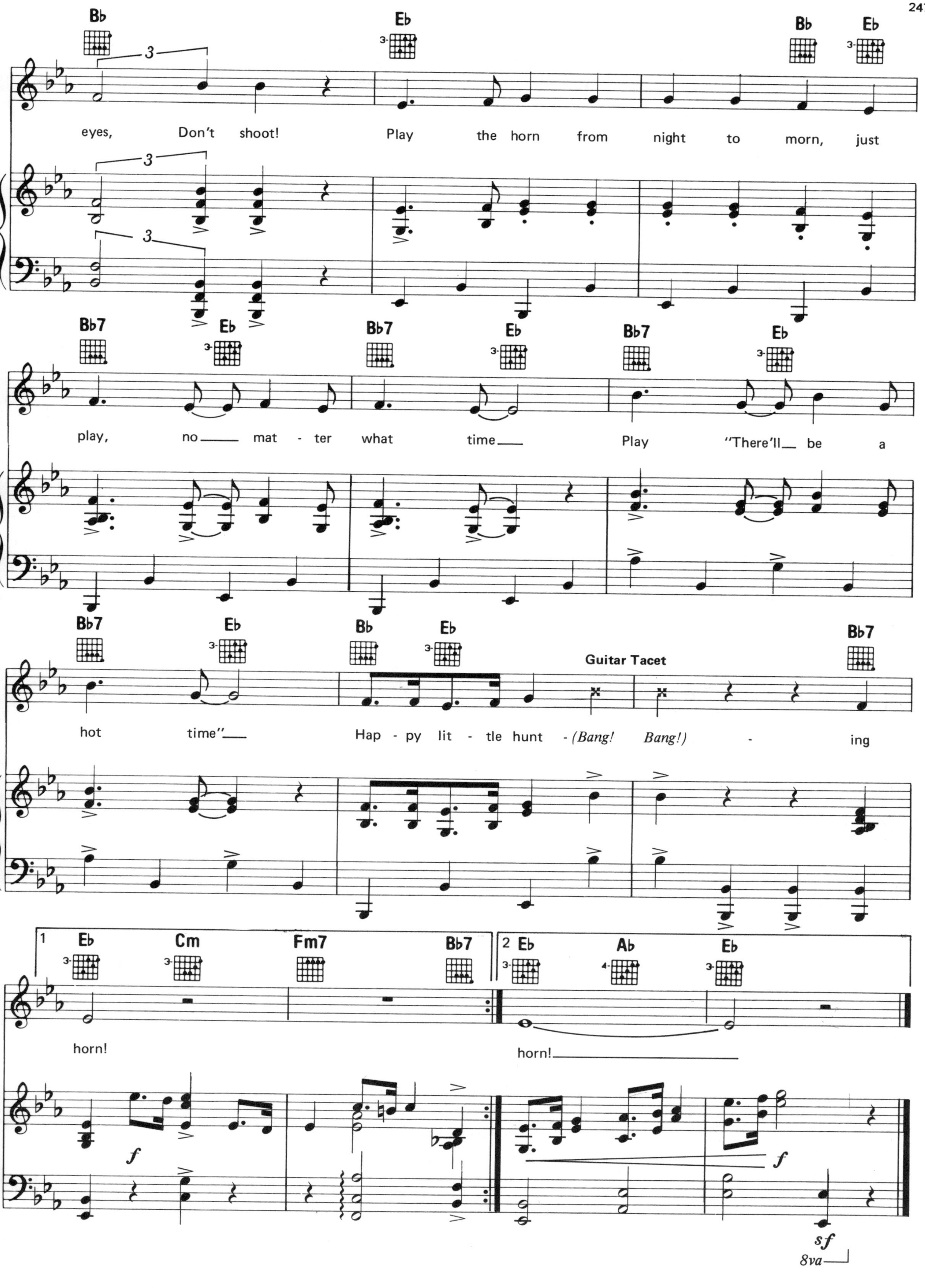
Bb
Eb
Bb
Eb
eyes, Don't shoot! Play the horn from night to morn, just
Bb7
Eb
Bb7
Eb
Bb7
Eb
play, no mat - ter what time Play "There'll be a
Bb7
Eb
Bb
Eb
Guitar Tacet
Bb7
hot time" Hap - py lit - tle hunt - (Bang! Bang!) - ing
1
Eb
Cm
Fm7
Bb7
2
Eb
Ab
Eb
horn!
horn!
f
f
sf
8va

You Took Advantage Of Me

Words by LORENZ HART
Music by RICHARD RODGERS

Gracefully
mf
p
He: In the spring when the feel-ing was chron-ic And my cau-tion was leav-ing you
She: When a girl has the heart of a moth-er It must go to some-one, of
flat I should have made use of the ton-ic Be-
course; It can't be a sis-ter or broth-er And
fore you gave me "that!" A men-tal de-fi-cient you'll
so I loved my horse. But hors-es are fre-quent-ly

E♭ B♭m7 E♭ E♭7+5 A♭ D7 Gm
grade me, I've giv - en you plen - ty of da - ta. You
sil - ly, Mine ran from the beach of Ka - lu - ta, And
C C7+5 F9(♭5) E♭ Bm6 B♭7
came, you saw and you slayed me, And that-a is that-a!
left me a - lone for a fil - ly, So I - a picked you-a.
L.H.
rit.
Refrain (liltingly)
E♭ E♮dim B♭7 E♭ E♭dim
I'm a sen - ti - men - tal sap, that's all. What's the use of try - ing
p a tempo
Fm7 B♭7 E♭dim E♭ E♭7 A♭ A♭m6
not to fall? I have no will, You've made your kill 'Cause you

Eb Eb+ Bb7 Eb B7 Bb7 Eb E♮dim
took ad - van-tage of me! I'm just like an ap-ple
Bb7 Eb Eb♮dim Fm7 Bb7 Eb♮dim
on a bough_ And you're gon-na shake me down some-how,_ So
Eb Eb7 Ab Abm6 Eb Eb+ Bb7 Eb Gm
what's the use,- you've cooked my goose_'Cause you took ad-van-tage of me!
Cm D7 G7 C7 F7 Bb7
I'm so hot and both-ered that I don't know_ My el-bow from_ my
mf

E♭ Cm D7 G7 C7
ear; I suf-fer some-thing aw-ful each time you go And
F7 B♭7 B♭ Fm7 B♭7 E♭ E♮dim
much worse when you're near. Here am I with all my
mp
B♭7 E♭ E♭dim Fm7 B♭7 E♭dim E♭ E♭7
bridg-es burned, Just a babe in arms where you're con-cerned, So lock the doors and
A♭ A♭m6 E♭ E♭+ B♭7 1. E♭ A♭6 B♭7 2. E♭
call me yours 'Cause you took ad-van-tage of me! me!

He Was Too Good To Me

By RICHARD RODGERS and LORENZ HART

Moderately
Fm Bb
There goes my young in -
Eb Fm Bb Eb
tend - ed, The thing is end - ed, re - grets are vain.
Fm Bb Eb Db Bb C7 B A Gb Ab
I'll nev - er find an - oth - er half so sweet, And we'll nev - er meet a -

Db Fm Bb Eb C7 Fm Cm6 Abmaj7
gain. I was a good sport, Told him Good-bye, Eyes dim, But why com-
accel.
Slowly with feeling
Bb7 Eb Fm6 Ab Gm Fm Bb7
plain? He was too good___ to me. How can I get a - long now?
rit.
p – mf
Eb Fm6 Ab Gm Fm Bb7 Eb
So close he stood___ to me, Ev' - ry - thing seems all wrong now! He would have
Abm Eb F7 Bb7 Eb Ebm6 Bb F7
brought me the sun.___ Mak - ing me smile___ That was his

Bb Ab Eb Bb7 Eb Fm6 Ab Gm
fun! When I was mean to him He'd nev - er say, "Go
Fm Bb7 Eb Fm7 Eb Fm6 Ab Gm Fm Bb7
'way now." I was a queen to him, Who's goin' to make me gay now?
Eb Abm Eb F7 Abm6 Eb Cm Fm7
It's on - ly nat - 'ral I'm blue ooo, He was too good
Bb9 1 Eb Cm6 Abmaj7 Bb7 2 Eb Abmaj7 Eb
to be true. true.
rall.
a tempo
cresc.
dim.
Ped.

Ten Cents A Dance

Music by RICHARD RODGERS
Lyric by LORENZ HART

In moderate tempo
mf
p
leggiero grazioso
E♭ Cm Fm7 B♭7 E♭ Cm Fm7 B♭7
I work at the Pal-ace Ball-room, But, gee, that pal-ace is cheap; When
E♭ Cm Gm Cm Gm Fm7 B♭7 E♭ B♭7
I get back to my chil-ly hall room I'm much too tir-ed to sleep, I'm
E♭ Cm Fm7 B♭7 E♭ Cm Gm
one of those la-dy teach-ers, A beau-ti-ful host-ess, you know, One

C7 F7 Eb F7 F7♭5 Fm7 Bb7
that the pal-ace fea-tures At ex-act-ly a dime a throw.
poco rit.
Refrain (slowly, quasi rubato)
Eb F♯dim Fm7 Bb7 Eb F7
Ten cents a dance; That's what they pay me. Gosh, how they weigh me
p-mf
Bb7 Eb F♯dim Fm7 Bb7
down! Ten cents a dance, Pan-sies and rough guys,
Eb7 Ab Dm7 G7 C7(♭9) Fm
Tough guys who tear my gown! Sev-en to mid-night, I hear drums,

C7(♭9) Fm D7 Gm
Loud-ly the sax - o-phone blows, Trum-pets are tear - ing my ear-drums.
poco cresc.
C7(♭9) F7 B♭7 E♭ F♯dim Fm7 B♭7
Cus-tom-ers crush my toes. Some-times I think I've found my he-ro
mf
p
E♭7 A♭ Dm7 G7 C7(♭9) A♭m6
But it's a queer ro - mance, All that you need is a tick-et;
E♭ E♭aug A♭maj7 E♭7(♭5) 1. B♭7 E♭ B♭5♯ 2. B♭7 E♭
Come on, big boy, ten cents a dance! ten cents a dance!
mf
f
8

PATTER
Cm G+ Cmi7 Cmi6 Eb Bb7
Fight-ers and sail-ors and bow-leg-ged tai-lors Can pay for their tick-ets and
p
Eb Cm G+ Cmi7 Cmi6
rent me! Butch-ers and bar-bers and rats from the har-bors Are
Eb Bb5# Eb Gm Eb7 C Eb7
sweet-hearts my good luck has sent me. Though I've a cho-rus of
mp
Gm Eb7 C7 Am F7 D F7 Am F7 D7
el-der-ly beaux, Stock-ings are por-ous with holes at the toes.

Gm Ebm6 Bb
I'm here till clos-ing time, Dance and be mer-ry, it's
F7 Bb7 Eb F#dim Fm7 Bb7
on-ly a dime. Some-times I think I've found my he-ro
mf sf mf
Eb Fmi7 Eb Dm7 G7 Edim C7
But it's a queer ro-mance, All that you need is a
Abm6 Eb Eb+5 Ab Eb7(-5) Gm Bb7 Eb
tick-et! Come on, big boy, ten cents a dance!
p mf cresc. f molto rit. sf

With A Song In My Heart

Words by LORENZ HART
Music by RICHARD RODGERS

Lively
mp
Eb
Ebm7
Eb7
He: Though I know that we meet ev - 'ry night And we
She: Oh, the moon's not a moon for a night; And these
p
Ab
Eb
Cm
could - n't have changed since the last time, To my joy and de - light it's a
stars will not twin - kle and fade out! And the words in my ears will re -
Fm7
Bb7
Eb
Ab
Eb
Ab
Eb
new kind of love at first sight.
sound for the rest of my years.
Though it's you and it's I all the
In the morn - ing I'll find with de -
p

B♭m7 E♭7 A♭ C♭
time Ev-'ry meet-ing's a mar-vel-ous pas-time, You're in-
light Not a note of our mu-sic is played out, It will
E♭ Cm Fm7 B♭7 E♭ A♭ E♭ E7 B♭7 B♭7+
creas-ing-ly sweet, So when-ev-er we hap-pen to meet
be just as sweet, And an air that I'll live to re-peat: I greet you
rall.
Refrain (rather slow but in steady rhythm)
E♭ B♭7 E♭
With a song in my heart. I be-hold your a-
p with great warmth
B♭7 E♭ G7
dor-a-ble face, Just a song at the start,
R.H.

Cm G7 Cm Cm7 Cm6
But it soon is a hymn to your grace. When the mu-sic swells
mp cresc.
Ab Fm7 Eb6 D7
I'm touch-ing your hand; It tells that you're
Fm D7 G7 C7 Fm Bb7 Eb
stand-ing near, and At the sound of your
mf dim. p
Bb7 Eb Bb7
voice Heav-en op-ens its por-tals to me.

Eb
G7
Cm
Can I help but re - joice
That a song such as
G7
Cm
Cm7
Cm6
F7
Eb
ours came to be?
But I al- ways knew
I would live life
mp
espressivo
cresc.
F7
Eb
Fm7
Bb7
1. Eb
Ebdim Eb
through
With a song in my heart for you.
f
più espr. e rall.
a tempo
mf espr.
E7
Bb7
Bb7+(b9)
2. Eb
you.
mf
p
Ped.

Blue Moon

Words by LORENZ HART
Music by RICHARD RODGERS

Calmly
mf
mp
poco rit.
Cm Cm7 F7 Fdim Cm G7 Cm
Once up-on a time, be-fore I took up smil-ing, I hat-ed the moon-light!
Once up-on a time My heart was just an or-gan, My life had no mis-sion.
p
Fm6 G7 Cm Cm7 F7 Fdim
Shad-ows of the night that po-ets find be-guil-ing seemed
Now that I have you, to be as rich as Mor-gan is
mf
p
Cm G7 Cm Fm G7 Cm Fm Dm7 G7
flat as the noon-light. With no one to stay
my one am-bi-tion. Once I a-woke at
mf
mp

Cmaj9 C6 Dm7 G7 C(D) C
up for I went to sleep at ten.
sev - en Hat - ing the morn - ing light.
Fm7 Bb7 Ebmaj7 Eb6 Cm7 F7 Fm7 Bb7
Life was a bit - ter cup for the sad - dest of all men.
Now I a - wake in Heav - en and all the world's all right.
rit.
Refrain (slowly, with feeling)
Bb7 Eb Cm Fm7 Bb7 Eb Cm
Blue Moon you saw me stand - ing a - lone
p
Fm Bb7 Eb Cm Fm7
With - out a dream in my heart, With - out a love of my own;

E♭ A♭ E♭ B♭7 E♭ Cm Fm7 B♭7
Blue Moon you knew just what I was there
E♭ Cm Fm7 B♭7 E♭ Cm Fm7
for you heard me say-ing a pray'r for some-one I real-ly could care
E♭ A♭ E♭ A♭ B♭7
for And then there sud-den-ly ap-peared be-
mf
E♭ A♭6 B♭7 E♭
fore me The on-ly one my arms will ev-er hold I heard some-

A♭m D♭7 G♭ B♭ Cm7 F7
bod-y whis-per "Please a - dore me" And when I looked, the moon had turned to
Fm7 B♭7 E♭ Cm Fm7 B♭7 E♭ Cm
gold! Blue Moon! Now I'm no long-er a - lone
p
Fm7 B♭ E♭ Cm Fm7
With-out a dream in my heart, With-out a love of my own.
1. E♭ A♭ E♭ B♭7 2. E♭ A♭ E♭
Blue
mf
Ped.

'Cause We Got Cake

Words by LORENZ HART
Music by RICHARD RODGERS

Moderately bright, with a lilt
mf
F
E♭/F
F
The spir - it's al - ways will - ing when it's fed.
B♭
C7
F
F6
When it's not fed the spir - it's dead.
F
E♭/F
F
And if the spir - it real - ly wants to dance,

Bb C7 F F6
It needs a lit - tle more than bread.
Am D9 G7 Cmaj9 C6 Cmaj7
To cure the spir - it's ache,
Am D9 G7 Bb/C Am/C Cdim C7
Give it a lit - tle cake!
F F6 F7/A Bb Gm7 Abdim
Come you all, kick up the cake walk, 'Cause we got cake,

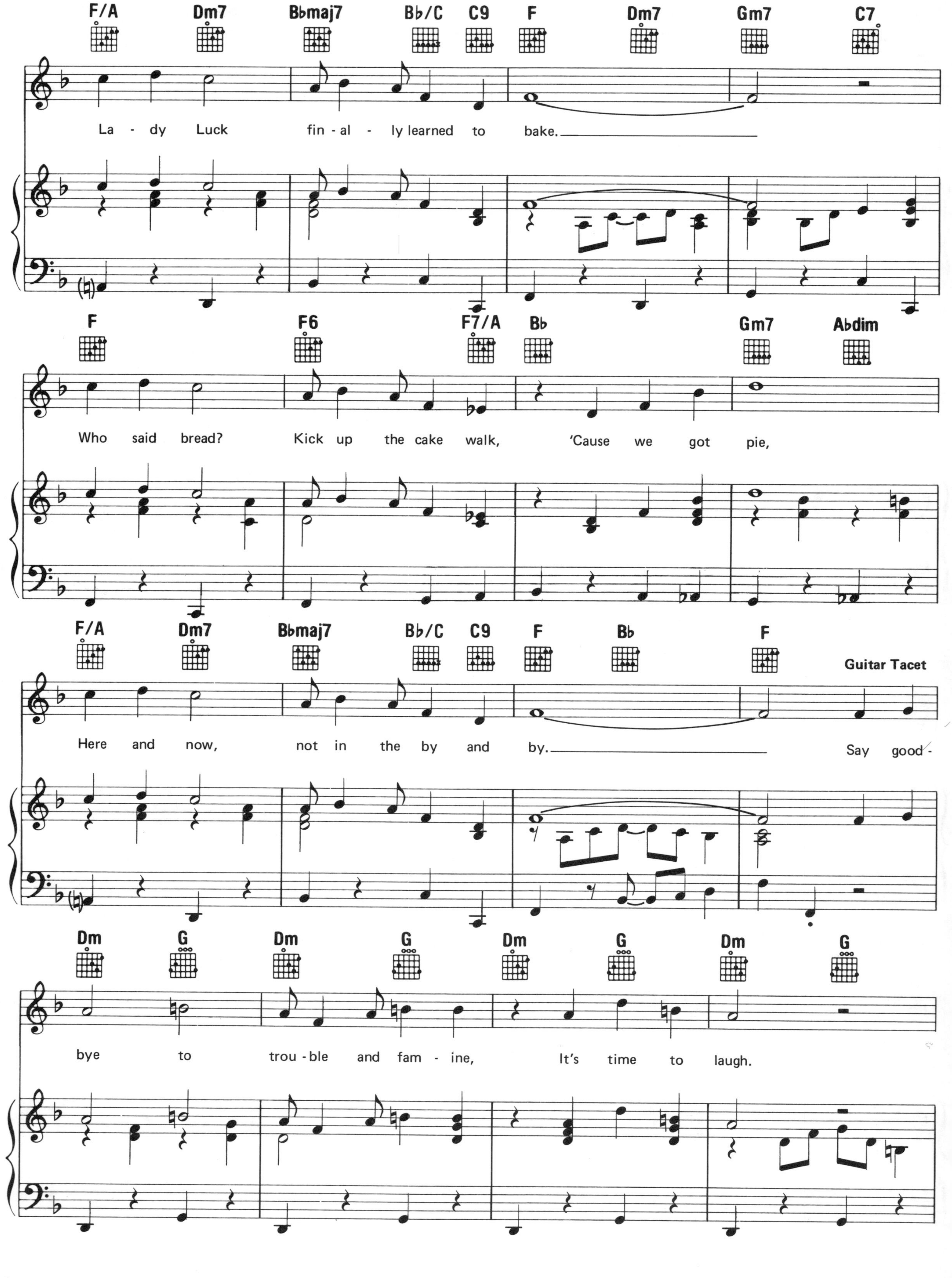
F/A Dm7 B♭maj7 B♭/C C9 F Dm7 Gm7 C7
La - dy Luck fin - al - ly learned to bake.
F F6 F7/A B♭ Gm7 A♭dim
Who said bread? Kick up the cake walk, 'Cause we got pie,
F/A Dm7 B♭maj7 B♭/C C9 F B♭ F
Guitar Tacet
Here and now, not in the by and by. Say good -
Dm G Dm G Dm G Dm G
bye to trou - ble and fam - ine, It's time to laugh.

Cm F Cm F Cm Bbm7-5
Laugh, boys, you can ex - am - ine the fat - ted calf.
F F6 F7/A Bb Gm7 Abdim
Come you all, kick up the cake walk, We got a break.
F/A Dm7 Bbmaj7 Gm7 C7-9 F/A D7+5
Ev' - ry - one who is a - wake walk, The cake walk,
G9 C7 1 F Gm C7 2 F Gbmaj7 F
'Cause we all got cake. cake.
f

I Didn't Know What Time It Was

Words by LORENZ HART
Music by RICHARD RODGERS

Moderately
mf
poco rit.
G6 D C D G6 D
Once I was young, yes-ter-day, per-haps, Danced with Jim and Paul And
p a tempo
C D G6 D C D
kissed some oth-er chaps. Once I was young, but nev-er was na-ïve, I
G D7 G B7+ B7 E7+
thought I had a trick or two up my im-ag-i-nar-y sleeve.

E7 A7-♭5 D7 Dm7 G Dm7 G
And now I know I was na - ïve!
p
Refrain (slowly and tenderly)
F♯m7 B7 Em F♯m7 B7
I did - n't know what time it was, Then I met
p
A Am Em Bm
you. Oh, what a love - ly time it was,
C Bm Am Dm7 D7 F♯m7 B7
How sub - lime it was, too! I did - n't

Em F♯m7 B7 A Am
know what day it was. You held my hand, Warm like the
Em Bm C Bm Am7 Dm D7
month of May it was, And I'll say it was grand.
G Am B7 Am B7
Grand to be a - live, to be young, to be mad, to be yours a -
mf più espressivo
Em C D7 Gmaj7
lone! Grand to see your face, feel your touch, hear your

Em7 A7 Am7 Dm7 D7 F♯m7 B7 Em
voice say I'm all your own! I didn't know what year it was,
F♯m7 B7 A Am Em Bm
Life was no prize. I want-ed love and here it was
C Bm Am7 Cm G B7 C6 D7 C6
Shin-ing out of your eyes. I'm wise and I know what time it is
1. G Em6 D7 2. G G6
now! now!
p
mf
f
Ped.

I Like To Recognize The Tune

Words by LORENZ HART
Music by RICHARD RODGERS

Moderato
mf
dim.
L.H.
F C F C7 F C7 F Bb C
Some fun - ny folks like to shoot off rock - ets, Oth - ers like to
mp a tempo
Bb C F C7 F C F C7 F
pick your pock - ets, Some of them kill when they feel the urge,
Bb F C7 F F6
Oth - ers go in for per - ju - ry.
mf

Am Dm Gm7 C
I too have a pas - sion that I can't un - der - stand; It
p
Dm G7 C F C7
comes out when I hear a band.
Guitar tacet
Gm7 C7 F6 F Gm7 C7
I like to rec - og - nize the tune, I want to sav - vy what the band is
p - mf
Dm Adim Bb6 Bbm6 F C7
play - ing, I keep say - ing Must you bur - y the

F Gm7 C7 F6 F
tune? I've got to know the an - swer soon, Is it a
Gm7 C7 Dm Adim Bb6 Bbm6
cat mee-ow - ing in the at - tic? Is it stat - ic?
F C7 F D7 G6
Must you bur - y the tune? A well known
mf
D7 G6 Am7 D7 Bb6
drum - mer plays the drums like thun - der, But the

F7 Bb G7 Bb C7
Guitar Tacet
mel - o - dy is six feet un - der. There is - n't
p
Gm7 C7 F6 F Gm7 C7
an - y one im - mune, They kill the Bil - ly Ros - es and Puc -
Dm Adim Bb6 Bbm6
ci - nis. Don't be mean - ies,
F C7 1 F 2 F
Guitar tacet
Must you bur - y the tune? I like to tune?
mf
sf

You're Nearer

Words by LORENZ HART
Music by RICHARD RODGERS

Moderately
mf
f
poco rit.
C
p a tempo
Time is a heal - er, but it can - not heal my heart, My
Dm/C
G7
mind says I've for - got - ten you and then I feel my heart, The
C
miles lie be - tween us, but your fin - gers touch my own, You're

Dm/C
C#dim
Dm7
nev - er far a - way from me, For you're too much my own.
G7-9
C
Cmaj7
C6
Dm7
G7
You're near - er than my head is to my pil - low,
p mf
Dm7
G7
C
Cmaj7
C6
Near - er than the wind is
Dm7
G7
Dm7
G7
C
to the wil - low, Dear - er
mf

D7 G7 E7 Am Am7
than the rain is to the earth be - low,
mf
D7 Gmaj7 C F Fmaj7
Prec - ious as the sun to the things that grow.
mp
mf
Dm7 G7-9 C Cmaj7 C6
You're near - er than the i - vy
p
Dm7 G7 Dm7 G7 C
to the wall is, Near - er
mf

D7 G7 E7 Bm7 E7
than the win - ter to the fall is,
mf
Am Am7 D7 C
Leave me, but when you're a - way You'll
Abm6 C Em Dm7 G7
know You're near - er for I love you
1 C G7-9
2 C
so. You're so.
f
mf
rall.
3
p

Give It Back To The Indians

Words by LORENZ HART
Music by RICHARD RODGERS

Pompously
mf
slowly
G D7b5 G D7b5 G D7b5 G D7b5 G D7b5 G D7b5
Old Peter Min-u-it had noth-ing to loose, When he bought the Isle of Man-
mf well marked
G G D7b5 G D7b5 G D7b5 G D7b5
hat-tan For twen-ty six Dol-lars and a bot-tle of booze And they
G D7b5 G D7b5 G B♮ F♯7 B F♯7
threw in the Bronx and Sta-ten. Pete thought that he had the

B F♯7 B F♯7 B F♯7 B F♯7 B D7
best of the bar-gain, But the poor red man just grinned. And
G D7♭5 G D7♭5 G D7♭5 G D7♭5 G D7♭5 G D7♭5
he grunt-ed "Ugh!" mean-ing O. K. in his Jar-gon, For he knew poor Pete was
G C Bm Am G C G Am
skinned. We've tried to run the Cit-y, But the Cit-y ran a-way! And
mf
faster
B6 Bmaj7
now, Pe-ter Min-u-it,

D6
D7
We can't con - - tin - ue it!
f
Refrain (brightly)
Gm
Broad-way's turn-ing in-to Con - ey, Cham-pagne Char-lie's drink-ing gin, -
mp
D7+
Gm
D7
Old New York is new and phon - ey, Give it back to the In - di - ans.
mf
Gm
Two cents more to smoke a Luck - y, Dodg- ing buss - es keeps you thin. -
mp

Gm D7+ Gm Guitar tacet
New New York is sim- ply duck- y, Give it back to the In - di - ans. Take all the
D7 Gm
reds, On the box- es made for soap.
mf
D7 Gm Gm6 Gm (maj7) Gm
Whites, on Fifth Av - en - ue,
C7 Fm
Blues down in Wall Street los - ing hope.

E7
E7(♭5)
A7(♭5)
D7
Big bar - gain to - day, Chief, take_ it a - way!
cresc.
f
Gm
Come, you bust-ed Cit - y slick - ers, Bet-ter take it on the chin._
mp
D7+
Fa-ther Knick has lost his knick - ers, Give it back to the In - - - di -
1. Gm Gm6 Am7 D7(♭9)
2. Gm D7 Gm
ans!
ans!
f
f

Any Old Place With You ■ At The Roxy Music Hall ■ Bewitched ■ Blue Moon ■ Blue Room ■ Bye And Bye ■ Can't You Do A Friend A Favor ■ 'Cause We Got Cake ■ College On Broadway ■ Come And Tell Me ■ Dancing On The Ceiling ■ Disgustingly Rich ■ Ev'rybody Loves You ■ Ev'rything I've Got ■ Falling In Love With Love ■ The Girl Friend ■ Give It Back To The Indians ■ Glad To Be Unhappy ■ Happy Hunting Horn ■ Have You Met Miss Jones? ■ He Was Too Good To Me ■ Here In My Arms ■ I Could W… Know What Time It Was ■ I Like To Recognize The Tune ■ I Married An Angel ■ I Wish I Were In Love Again ■ I'd Rather Be Right ■ I've Got Five Dollars ■ I've Gotta Get Back To New York ■ Isn't It Romantic? ■ It Never Entered My Mind ■ It's A Lovely Day For A Murder ■ It's Easy To Remember ■ It's Got To Be Love ■ Johnny One Note ■ Jupiter Forbid ■ The Lady Is A Tramp ■ Little Girl Blue ■ Love Me Tonight ■ Lover ■ Manhattan ■ Mimi ■ Moon Of My Delight ■ The Most Beautiful Girl In The World ■ Mountain Greenery ■ My Funny Valentine ■ My Heart Stood Still ■ My Romance ■ Nobody's Heart ■ On A Desert Island With Thee ■ Quiet Night ■ Sentimental Me ■ A Ship Without A Sail ■ Sing For Your Supper ■ Soon ■ Spring Is Here ■ Ten Cents A Dance ■ There's A Small Hotel ■ This Can't Be Love ■ This Funny World ■ Thou Swell ■ To Keep My Love Alive ■ A Tree In The Park ■ Wait Till You See Her ■ Where Or When ■ Where's That Rainbow? ■ Who Are You? ■ With A Song In My Heart ■ You Are Too Beautiful ■ You Mustn't Kick It Around ■ You Took Advantage Of Me ■ You're Nearer

U.S. $19.95

ISBN 0-88188-337-9

0 73999 29560 3

HL00307940

HAL•LEONARD